THE NEW FACE OF GRAND PARENTING

why parents need their own parents

THE **NEW FACE** OF **GRAND** PARENTING

why
parents
need
their
own
parents

DON SCHMITZ

The New Face of Grandparenting . . . Why Parents Need Their Own Parents
©2004 by Donald E. Schmitz

Published by:
Grandkidsandme
1764 Hampshire Ave.
St. Paul, MN 55116
USA

Website: www.grandkidsandme.com
Email: book@grandkidsandme.com
Phone: 651-695-1988

Cover design: Dunn + Associates Design
Cover photo:
Book design & typesetting: Liz Tufte, Folio Bookworks

All photos ©Donald E. Schmitz

Publishers Cataloging-in-Publication Data

Schmitz, Don.
The new face of grandparenting : why parents need their own parents /
Don Schmitz. -- 1st ed. -- St. Paul, MN : Grandkidsandme, 2003.
    p. ; cm.
Includes bibliographical references and index.
    ISBN: 0-9741710-0-X

1. Grandparenting. 2. Grandparents and child. 3. Family.
4. Interpersonal relations. I. Title.
HQ759.9 .S36 2003
306.874/5—dc22   0311

SAN -255-3902
Printed in the U.S.A.

A note to the reader

This book is written for parents, grandparents, and great-grandparents to help successfully parent and grandparent in the 21st century. My hope is this book will support and encourage greater involvement in today's complex, changing configuration of family.

I ask that you take to heart the important roles you play in the lives of your children and grandchildren. Realize that the simple things that you do today will have a profound effect on your families and future generations. The well being of our complicated world requires your involvement.

> "My grandmother would tell me stories, and now I realize her voice is my voice and the two of us have become one."
> — *Kay Harvey, grandmother and reporter for the St. Paul Pioneer Press*

Acknowledgments

This book would not have been written without the mentorship of my mother-in-law Mary Marso.

I thank the following people for their contributions to this book: Richard Brooke, Ruth Meyer Brown, Shirley Cavallaro, Paul Child, Carol Ernste, James Fuchs, Carole Gesme, Robert Grodahl, Jerry Kind, Tom Maus, Suzanne McGann, Dorothy Michels, Tina Miller, Pat Morris, Cheryl Mozey, Kate O'Keefe, Dianne Pettet, Laurie & Floyd Ott, Marce & Steve Piller, Mary Regnier, Andrew & Kari Schmitz, Norma & Larry Schuh, Cecilia Sorenson, Erma Wachtler, Diane Westendorp and Judy Wolf.

A special thanks goes to Jeanne Doyle for her countless hours of taking my words and putting them into this meaningful book.

Contents

Introduction

The passion behind the vision

I am often asked why I started Grandkidsandme. It's a thought-provoking question and I am happy to say I had a special mentor. Her name was Mary and she was a wonderful grandmother to my three sons, but most of all she was a wonderful mother-in-law. She believed in me and recognized that my skills were underdeveloped and took me under her wing. It's no wonder my definition of grandparenting is "someone who supports the dreams of grandchildren."

Grandkidsandme was created as a direct outcome of my experiences as a child. My maternal grandparents had thirty-six grandchildren and little time to spend with their grandchildren. My grandfathers are only a faint memory and the only memory I have of my paternal grandmother was her anger, when my brother and I unlocked the piano with a coffee key. Only recently did I learn that my great-grandfather had sold his prize team of horses so that his daughters could play that piano.

My parents have seven children and twenty-three grandchildren. After their children had grown and left home to live on their own, my parents, welcomed no longer being "parents."

It was after I had three children, I learned how valuable

grandparents could be. My father-in-law died within a year of our marriage, but my mother-in-law made it a priority to love our children and share in their young lives. Grandma Mary came to visit often and shared in many childhood experiences: from new teeth, holidays, learning to walk, to riding a bike. Unfortunately, she died only a few years later, before my oldest son was nine.

My time with Grandma Mary was indeed too short, but her effect remains with me today. I had the opportunity to be understudy to a special mentor. Mary left a lasting impact on her grandchildren and the adult children in her life.

The expectations placed on parents today can quickly become overwhelming. No one truly understands what he or she is getting into when they become a parent; yet most parents are reluctant to ask for help. After all, you raised them to be self sufficient and independent. The reality is that parents need all the help they can get and, in most cases, their own parents, the grandparents of their children, are willing and able to provide it.

Grandparenting is a great excuse to re-establish yourself with your adult children and at the same time provide you with endless opportunities to enhance the lives of your grandchildren. Grandparenting provides a wonderful avenue to forge meaningful relationships in the lives of the next generation. It is my hope that other grandparents will be motivated by this book to become more involved in the lives of their children and grandchildren.

The vision of Grandkidsandme is to rekindle the spirit of grandparenting within the family and to offer new or renewed ways for 21st century grandparents to have a positive influence in their grandchildren's lives.

My vision for the future of family

- Grandparents will take an active role in the lives of their grandchildren.

- Children will look to their parents for support.

- Parents will learn to forgive their parents.

- Grandparents will be open to learning and change.

- Grandparents and parents will learn to trust their love for each other and accept and appreciate their differences.

- Parents will consider the long-term effects their actions will have on their children.

- Grandparents will take time to play with and learn from their grandchildren.

- Parents will live as caring, ethical and moral examples for their children.

- Grandparents will be present and accessible.

- Children will continue to ask questions of adults and discover their own solutions.

- Parents will nurture self-love in their children.

- Grandparents will be examples of how to live a life well.

- Grandparents will recognize they are emerging beings that are continuing to grow.

- Parents will respect their own parents and their children.

- Grandparents will use the gifts of perspective and life experiences to teach their grandchildren.

- Children will be better people by emulating the lives of parents and grandparents.

- Grandparents will lovingly share songs, talents, time, and wisdom with all who listen.

- Society will look to our aging population as a vital resource for stability in our culture.

Bringing Generations Together

1

The changing family

The history

In the 1800s, immigrants came to this country from all over the world. They left their homes in search of new opportunities in America, risking great danger for newfound freedoms. Their decision to come across miles of ocean required courage and sacrifice. They were forced to leave much behind: parents, relatives, customs, language and earthly possessions. They came to create new opportunities for their families and many died in their attempt to realize their dreams. The families who survived were forced to make dramatic changes, but managed to raise their families, establish businesses and provide food for a growing nation.

The Industrial Revolution forced many young families to leave the family farm and move to the city: leaving parents and relatives behind. Our cities evolved into home for millions of people and the family structure was forever altered. Fathers worked long hours away from home and mothers assumed the primary care for the children. Though multiple generations were no longer living under the same roof, relatives usually made their homes within a short distance of one another. Grandparents were usually close-by with full cookie jars, advice and a willingness to help.

The advent of Social Security brought the next significant change. During the 1930–1950s, Social Security brought with it a mandatory retirement age of sixty-five and a steady income for life. For the first time in history, Americans were assured of a time when they would no longer have to work. In return for a monthly check, they could retire, freeing job opportunities for younger workers. Prior to 1900, only four percent of the workforce ever retired. Senior citizens who could no longer work lived with their children out of financial necessity. With a steady income from Social Security, retirees could afford to remain in their own homes and live independently of their children.

After World War II, returning servicemen generated the baby boom and corresponding economic boom. Young couples wanted more space for their growing families and because the average family could afford an automobile, suburbs sprang up across the country. Young families flocked to these new neighborhoods, while grandma and grandpa remained in the city.

According to the 2000 U.S. Census, until the 1960s, "The average American family was made up of 3.2 children. A father who was the primary breadwinner for the family and a mother, who was responsible for the housework, cared for the children, and provided voluntary contributions of time and energy to church and community." The '60s brought the women's movement, smaller families and another change in the family. At the same time, medical science developed reliable birth control, and technology invented modern appliances. Almost simultaneously, women were no longer tied to long hours of housework. They could decide when and how many children they wanted and were encouraged to enter the work force.

As women entered the work force, childcare became an

industry. Day care centers and latchkey programs became big business. Whether corporate centered or home-based, for the first time in American history non-family members provided a large percentage of pre-school childcare.

Today, your family may live across the street, across the continent, or halfway around the world. As our families spread throughout the country and the world, the need for family connections have become even more important as the physical space between them increases.

The look of "family" has changed. Many families look quite different than they did a generation ago, and would be almost unrecognizable to those who lived in the last century. Divorce, adoptions, single women choosing to be mothers, gay and lesbian couples becoming parents has also changed the faces of family portraits.

The events of September 11th rekindled an awareness of the importance of family and a reconnection in many families. It is too early to know how this tragedy will affect families over time. Shortly after September 11th, the interaction between friends and neighbors increased. Families are turning to their immediate and extended families. It's a wonderful example of grass roots participation out from under the umbrella of a government program. Not only does our decision to increase our involvement help families, but also ourselves.

The financial ramifications triggered by September 11th are also having an effect. The Investment Company Institute reports that since September 11, 2001, and the subsequent recession, many seniors are putting off retirement or even returning to work after watching slumping stock prices take a bite out of their retirement income. Reductions in government spending and increases in the cost of health coverage are leaving many Americans with but one choice: work more years, longer hours at current jobs or find additional part time work. Once again, families are being threatened.

This book explores some of the changes in family relationships, shares research gathered from Grandpa, Grandma and Parent Focus Groups and provides insights and ideas for parents and grandparents. Along the way, the author shares personal experiences as a teacher and the knowledge gained in working with Grandkidsandme® Camps and Grandkid Days.®

The author's experience as a father, grandfather and educator will help us "Bring Generations Together."

2

Today's family:
How, where, who are we?

Today's parents, committed and challenged

Parents receive little praise and less credit for doing a good job as parents. A 2002 survey conducted by the YMCA and the Search Institute found that most important thing people could do to support parents was to reassure them. "Others telling me I'm doing a good job as a parent," was a frequent response in the survey.

A young father's comment demonstrates that our children need support, "I am sometimes confused about my role. The rules have changed and the lack of role models has shaken my confidence. Much is expected of me both at home and at work."

Parents are caught up in the frenzy of today's busy schedules. Everyone seems to be in a hurry. Parents rush home from work to drive their children to soccer practice, using cell phones to confirm play dates, doctor appointments, softball practice, gymnastics, music and dance lessons, while waiting in line to order dinner at the drive-thru restaurant.

No parent wants to hear, "Your child is already behind. She should have started two years ago," or when a third grader wants to try out for basketball to be told, "He should have started in kindergarten if he wanted to be on the traveling team in fourth grade."

One hassled father's biggest fear was, "Someone saying to me that my child is behind. Our solution is to sign our children up for soccer, swimming lessons and gymnastics. We run ourselves ragged trying to make it happen. It's a cycle we don't know how to break."

Many parents believe they must live at this speed in order to feel productive and do the "best for our children." These fears make parents anxious and guilt-ridden, so they register their children for all kinds of activities, even when the child may not be interested.

Parents get caught up in the guilt trip of what they perceive other parents are doing. "I feel such pressure to have my child participate in organized activities. I just want to hide when I tell my friends that I'm not having my daughter try out for soccer." Several grandparents commented on the busy schedules that their grandchildren have today; "It's getting so that the only time I get to see my grandson is on the baseball field."

One proactive grandmother sees the busy schedule as her opportunity for involvement: "The state of constant activity provides me with an opportunity to get involved. I can help by taking my granddaughter to her activities when my daughter is unavailable."

Mary and Ken have two children. Ken works full time for a large computer company and is trying to advance his career. Mary also works approximately thirty hours a week. Their two children, ages six and eight, arrive at their latchkey program at

7:00 AM, go to school until 3:00, then return to latchkey. Either Ken or Mary picks the children up between 5:30 and 6:00 four days a week. Two nights a week they eat sandwiches in the car on their way to karate lessons. T-ball and softball take up another night in the spring.

The kids go to bed at 8:30 PM. Other than the rush to get everyone ready in the morning, parents and children see each other all of three and a half hours a day at most and part of that time is occupied by other activities such as cooking, cleaning, yard work and homework. The children have little unstructured time and when they do, Mary and Ken are too tired to enjoy their own children.

A mother of a six-month-old baby signed her daughter up for swimming lessons and gymnastics. When asked why, she responded, "I felt by doing this, I was being a good parent."

We all need to establish our priorities and feel comfortable in doing so. Whose idea is it that our children's schedules should be so crazy? Are we trying to keep up with the neighbors? Why do we feel a need to whisper that we are not going to encourage our children to go out for sports? Why don't we feel ok about sitting down and having a dinner together as a family?

A few brave parents are trying to put a stop to the frenetic activities and are choosing to spend more time at home with their children. These families are making efforts to put the family first. Recently, I spoke to parents who decided they were going to make some changes at their house. They agreed that if the children didn't want to sign up for sports, they were no longer going to encourage them to do so. When they shared their decision with their son, they were shocked to hear him say, "I was only going to play baseball because you wanted me to." It's not only the parents who are feeling pressured.

Parents are hard on themselves and take a great deal of

blame when their children fail. They continually worry that they are not doing enough for their children. Parents must find ways to create balance in their lives and use the resources of their families and communities for support.

Peter's family lives in a suburban location in Florida. His family consists of his Japanese wife, Myoko and her mother, an adopted eight-year-old Korean daughter Alice, a biological four-year-old son, Jeff and a cat. Every three years, they travel to Japan to visit Myoko's extended family. Peter, who was born in Ohio, visits his mother once or twice a year. His father lives and works in California. Because of the distance from their parents and siblings, Peter and Myoko's "extended family" is made up of friends and neighbors. They regularly attend the YMCA where they are actively involved and attend a neighborhood church on occasion.

Peter works out of his home as a web site designer while Myoko travels one-third of the time as a flight attendant out of Detroit. Myoko's mother assists in caring for the children when Myoko is away working.

Peter and Myoko's family is not unusual, but it is not a "typical American family." The traditional family tree no longer adequately represents most families. A "salad bowl" might better describe today's family with its diverse contents.

The stress of childcare

According to the US Census Bureau, "Of the 41.8 million children under 15 who lived with two parents in 2002, more than 25 percent had mothers who did not work and stayed home." So who takes care of all the rest of the children? This figure is surprisingly down two percent from 1994. Part of the reason, I believe, is the lack of quality childcare in America.

Families are often forced to turn to private childcare when both parents are working, but it does not adequately provide for the needs of their children. Stanley Greenspan, M.D., a reputed scholar and leader in parenting, believes that out-of-home, non-parental childcare is in disarray and in need of immediate attention, noting that, according to the best studies, only nine to fifteen per cent of childcare is of high quality.

Childcare in America is in serious need of repair. According to Representative Bernie Sanders from Vermont, "The current childcare in this country is in crisis mode for working parents . . . childcare workers are grossly underpaid. Families that can afford quality childcare, pay an average of $5,500 per child annually." Childcare has one of the highest employee turnover rates of any profession. A widely held criticism of childcare is that the relationships created between the child and the caregivers are not long term. Children need stability and consistency in their lives, not constant change.

There are childcare alternatives available. Co-abode (www.co-abode.com) matches single mothers interested in sharing housing, play groups, baby-sitting co-ops and other parent support networks.

"For me, there's been a tremendous sense of relief in house sharing with another mom and her child," says Barbara, a single parent of two boys, Tyler, and Kevan. "At the end of the day we get together and tackle what has to be done: You do the dinner; I'll help the kids get their homework done. We have a mutual respect and admiration for each other. My kids have a playmate and are easier to manage. I now have more money to spend on them."

Co-abode provides a solution for financial problems as well as ease the loneliness of solo parenting. It provides creative alternatives to solving the need for quality childcare.

Jenny and Peter are a happily married two-income couple who are about to become parents. They live in a suburban community where several day care centers are relatively close. They spend a large percentage of their income on their home and two car payments.

Peter works for a small staffing firm and Jenny works for the local post office. Both Jenny and Peter enjoy their work and believe that in order to get ahead, they both must continue to work.

When Jenny has her baby, the postal service will provide twelve weeks of maternity leave without pay. She intends to use her maternity leave immediately after the baby is born and hopes to extend her leave for an additional month without pay.

Jenny and Peter checked with their respective employers about the possibility of working fewer hours and retaining their present positions. Jenny's employer will allow her to work part time, but she will lose all her benefits; something they can't afford to do. Peter's employer does not provide an alternative to his current full-time status.

They have considered the option of using family members for childcare. Jenny's parents live over a day's drive away and both work full time. Her sister, who lives nearby and stays home with her child, could be counted on to help. Peter's parents live a half-hour away.

What did Jenny and Peter do? Their solution was to have Jenny work part time and have her grandparents, her sister and one friend take care of their baby when Jenny is working. Peter's parents will also help two days a month.

This scenario is being played out daily across America. The solutions may be different and each unique situation requires a great deal of thought, planning and organization. Money plays a big part in the decision and none of these complicated solutions is ideal.

Friends and family have been providing assistance for generations. The vast majority of grandparents believe they have some responsibility to help their grandchildren and often provide long-term solutions. A survey conducted by AARP (American Association of Retired People) found, "Twenty-two percent of grandparents assist with childcare and approximately thirty-three percent of all grandparents care for one or more grandchildren each week."

An increasing number of grandparents are caring for their grandchildren when both parents are working. AARP's research found, "The number of families in which a grandparent is the caregiver makes up approximately eleven percent of the population." Grandparent help saves the family the expense of daycare as well as provides an opportunity for the grandchildren to know their grandparents.

Employers and the family

"Workers in the United States work the most hours of any country and have the shortest vacations," according to the University of Minnesota's Dr. William Doherty. The result of the long hours and few vacations is little quality for family time. Many parents find time only to eat, sleep and work. Working mothers continue to shoulder the brunt of raising the children in addition to working full time outside the home.

In 1993, the revised Family and Medical Leave Act by the U.S. Department of Labor provided up to twelve weeks of unpaid leave for a mother and father in any twelve-month period for the birth of a baby, providing the employee has worked for the company for at least one year. Since then, more than fifty percent of the states have passed legislation that deals with parental leave. California, in 2002, passed the first paid family leave of absence in the United States. According to a labor project at the University of California at Berkeley, "Beginning

July 1, 2004, workers will receive up to six weeks of paid leave per year to care for a new born (birth, adoption, or foster care) or seriously ill family member (parent, child, spouse, or domestic partner)." Employers are slowly increasing flexibility in the workplace but it remains to be seen if we will ever match many European countries in child benefits.

Stanley Greenspan, M.D., long recognized for his brilliant insights into emotional and intellectual development of infants, proposes the "Four-Thirds" solution for family care. His plan calls for "both parents to work two-thirds time and devote the remaining one-third to caring for their children." Greenspan does not mention grandparents as part of the "four-thirds" solution but if grandparents were part of his proposal, it could reduce the need for parents to work two full time jobs. The idea is very good in its purest form and could be used to stimulate the economy, especially if our country experiences a slow economy and high unemployment. Under Greenspan's proposal, two parents working two-thirds time would actually free up an additional half-time position, creating additional jobs. Unfortunately, the cost of Greenspan's proposal would be difficult for most businesses to implement.

Ideas & suggestions
for parents

1. Re-centering your thoughts about family

- Recognize that "never enough" goes with parenting and live with it.
- Accept the fact that children will bring disorder to your life.
- Be realistic in what you expect of yourself and your children.
- Take care of yourself.
- Find time to be alone.
- Create time for your partner.
- Work as a team in making decisions.
- Celebrate your successes.

2. Selecting childcare

Visit several children's sites. Survey a minimum of three childcare sites each year and use the following questions to compare the services provided:

- What is the experience of the staff?
- What is the ratio of adults to children?
- How clean is the facility and how often is it maintained?
- What food is provided?
- Is there evidence of discipline?
- Observe the materials and equipment and compare the materials to other sites.
- Observe lessons being taught. Are choices provided?

3. Changing childcare

Thinking about how childcare has changed; ask yourself the following questions:

- What is different?
- What is missing?
- What is better today?
- What alternatives in childcare are available?
- How can we add some of the missing ingredients?
- The activity must be in the home.
- The family will always be there to support one other.
- In-laws are a part of the family, as are significant others.
- Everyone is respectful of each other.

Ideas & suggestions
for grandparents

1. Growth and you

Each year the lobster goes out to sea and sheds its shell. Only then is it in position to grow again:

- What is keeping you from becoming all you can be?
- Are you in a position to grow?
- If age is not a barrier to personal growth, what is impeding you? One by one, examine any existing obstacles and create a plan.

2. A look at our childhood

Comparing your childhood with your adult children and grandchild can be an eye-opening experience:

- In what ways are your grandchildren's lives and your childhood alike?
- What is different?
- What was missing from your childhood?
- In what ways are your grandchildren better off than you were as a child?
- What do you think your grandchildren are missing today? Can you provide it?

This is a good story

3

Grandparents today

We all know grandparents whose values transcend passing fads and pressures and who possess the wisdom of distilled pain and joy. Because they are usually free to love and guide and befriend the young without having to take daily responsibility for them, they can often reach out past pride and fear of failure and close the space between generations.

— President Jimmy Carter

Grandparent-parent groups

For hundreds of years, the role of grandparents remained much the same. Today, the traditional roles of parents and grandparents are being replaced by a vast array of lifestyles as our culture continues to evolve.

As I prepared to write this book, I wanted to know: What do today's grandparents see as their roles in the family? What if anything has changed about their roles? Are their views similar or significantly different from those of their parents and adult children?

In addition to my reading and observations, I conducted research with three groups I called the "Parent Group," the "Grandma Group" and the "Grandpa Group." The response to questions and the discussions that occurred within these groups were extremely helpful in my gaining insights as to how each group perceives their roles and the roles of one another.

Research results

Though most of the grandparents and all of the parents were very much involved with their children and grandchildren, some grandparents did admit they were not involved at all.

As expected, the grandparents living close to their grandchildren saw their grandchildren more often than those living some distance apart. Most of the grandparents participating see their grandchildren each week and their distant grandchildren, those living over six hours away, twice a year. Phone calls, e-mails, letters and cards helped the grandparents bridge the distance and maintain connections between visits.

Parents see the grandparent's primary role as a resource for themselves and their children: "Someone who loves, supports and listens." The consensus was that the parent has the responsibility for the child all of the time; a grandparent is responsible for short periods of time. It also was agreed that grandparents serve as a sounding board for the parents and assist in reaffirming the boundaries parents have set for their children.

Speaking to the differences between the roles of parent and grandparent, one grandfather stated, "As a parent, I was overly strict and placed too much emphasis on things that honestly didn't matter in the overall picture. As a grandfather, I recognize more accurately what really matters; I can now apply that insight with my children and grandchildren." One parent offered her childhood memory: "My parents worried about me all the time. I used to love to go to my Grandma's and Grandpa's just to get away."

Charmaine Ciardi writes in her book The Magic of Grandparenting, "The average person becomes a grandparent between the ages of forty-five and fifty." If a grandparent lives to eighty-five years of age, they will have spent more than one-third of their life as a grandparent. Increased longevity, healthier lifestyles and cultural changes result in the grandparent of today bearing little resemblance to the grandparents they remember.

> "My grandparents taught me that it's not the activity that counts, it's the time together."
> — *Grandparent Group*

When surveying grandparents about the memories of their grandparents, most grandparents said they never knew their grandfathers and what they did remember about their grandparents was predominantly about their grandmothers. Others, when reminiscing about their grandparents, remembered a different way of life. "I remember having dinners at my grandparent's home. I also remember thinking how old they were and their simple devout life." A grandmother wrote, "My grandparents' home had a restful, quiet atmosphere that I enjoyed, even as a child. It made me feel secure, safe and happy. I loved sitting on the front porch with my grandmother, watching people pass by. Some would stop to chat. I never felt left out because everyone talked to me."

"They were warm and friendly and cared about me," said another grandfather. "I remember dinners with lots of family and playing in my grandparents' big house." Another grandmother remembers, "I didn't have grandparents, but I was very close to my two aunts. They always made me feel like the sun rose and set on me. It was a great comfort to know that my aunts loved me and would always be there for me."

Other memories included:

- "Visiting the farm, gathering eggs, driving the tractor and playing in the barn."
- "Talking around the big kitchen table."
- "Swimming at the lake with cousins."
- "My grandmother's loving voice."
- "Hanging out the laundry on the clothesline."
- "Picking vegetables from the garden."
- "Sitting with cousins and listening to Grandpa tell us stories."
- "Nicknames like, Bird, Stinkweed, Snitch, Punky, Blood Veins and Curly."
- "Cooking with my grandmother and the aromas of the kitchen."

Infant wisdom

Three-year-old Noah went out to the barn to see the new litter of kittens with his grandfather. On returning, Grandma said, "What did you see?"

Noah said, "I saw three kittens, two boys and one girl."

Grandma said, "So, how did you know if they were boy kittens or girl kittens?"

Noah replied, "Grandpa picked them up and looked underneath, I think it's stamped on their bottom."

Grandpa: then and now

For centuries, grandfathers have had little time to influence their grandchildren. Many died young or were forced to work too long. Today's younger healthier grandfathers have the opportunity to have a real impact on their grandchildren and the next generation.

> *Peter had always planned to retire at age sixty-five from his engineering position. His wife, Sarah, after finishing college at the age of forty-five, went to work in computer technology for a large airline company. They both saved the maximum in their 401K's and compiled a substantial retirement fund by the time they were fifty-five.*
>
> *Peter's plans ultimately changed and he retired at age fifty-five while Sarah chose to continue working. Peter enjoys spending time each week with one of his three grandchildren. He is challenging himself by learning to play the guitar and writing a book on his hobby, fly-fishing.*

The role of grandfathers and how they live their role, is the next significant influence boomer men will have on our culture. As women take on more of the economic responsibility for the family, the family's dependence on the father to provide for the financial resources is less demanding. Working mothers has given many middle-aged men the opportunity to pursue their interests, even change careers, something never dreamed of by their fathers and grandfathers.

> **"My grandpa tells good stories, even sometimes when you don't ask!"**
> — *Anonymous*

Grandparents, especially grandfathers, are a largely untapped resource available to young families. Many boomer grandfathers have different skills than their parents and grandparents. They were the first generation of men to help change diapers, do the laundry, help with grocery shopping and share cooking and cleaning chores. This experience provides them with a better understanding and comfort level with the day-to-day tasks and demands of a growing family. What they lack are role models to be the kind of grandfathers their grandchildren and children need.

As new parents learn how to parent, new grandparents are also learning their roles. Grandparents and their adult children should discuss and come to an understanding of the grandparent's roles. Grandparents should give serious thought to what kind of relationship they want to have with their grandchildren. It is the grandparent's responsibility to communicate what role they would like to have to their adult children. What that relationship will be is ultimately the parents' decision.

Who is grandma?

Today's mothers and grandmothers can be found in a wide variety of circumstances. Some remain at home while others have sought to work outside the home as physicians, teachers, pilots, presidents of corporations and entrepreneurs to name but a few. Some mothers are making the laws for our country and in our life time, one may be President of the United States.

The grandmothers of a century ago would be amazed at the changes in "woman's work." Today's woman is an expert at multitasking. She combines her career with being a wife, a mother, a grandmother, and often a caregiver to aging parents. She serves on boards and plays vital roles in her church and community.

Sarah is the head of a large family-owned business. She is also the mother of three children and grandmother of two. She lives in

Seattle, Washington, and her grandchildren live in California. She works full time in her twelve-year-old business. She wants to see her grandchildren as often as possible but has seen her two-year-old granddaughter only three times. Sarah has no intention of retiring as she enjoys both her work and her family and has created an effective balance between them. Sarah is a role model to many young mothers and fathers at her workplace. As CEO, she has helped to create flexibility for her employees and their families by revamping vacation, personal time and flex work schedules.

Kathy has chosen another way to balance her family and career life. The former head of human resources for a large company, Kathy, at the age of fifty-five, chose to exercise her option for early retirement and became a part-time caregiver for her three grandchildren. In order to do so, she sold her home in New York and moved to Chicago, where her grandchildren live. It was a very difficult decision, but she has few regrets. She loves watching her grandchildren grow and believes she has made the right decision for her grandchildren, her family and herself.

Jane began working full time when her children were in high school. She managed a research laboratory for a large medical company, working long hours for over twenty years. She and her husband divorced when she was forty-six and she never remarried. When she was fifty-nine, she chose to give up her management position to work part-time on her own research. Now, at sixty-seven, she has no plans to end her career but has reduced her hours. On her two days off each week, she spends one day shopping and playing golf and the other day is spent with her daughter, son-in-law and grandchildren.

Grandparents are important

Charmaine Ciardi, a grandparent expert, says, "We are witnessing a resurgence of interest in grandparenting and, most especially, in the unique power inherent in the grandparent-grandchild relationship." Grandparents have a natural position in the family to provide unconditional love, care and comfort to their grandchildren. At the same time, they can provide the support their adult children need.

> "As a child, I viewed the time with my grandparents as a treat. They were the ones who spent special time with me."
> — *Parent Group*

Arthur Kornhaber, a leading expert on grandparenting and author of *The Grandparent Guide,* identifies the following as some of the ways grandparents contribute to the family: living ancestors, family historians, mentors, nurturers, and role models.

Today's boomer grandparents have the opportunity to define their roles and create a new grandparent model that mirrors their changing lifestyles, yet supports the needs of their children, families and grandchildren.

Whether or not it is relearning how to care for a newborn, helping during a crisis, or a sympathetic ear to listen to the concerns of a stressed-out, exhausted mother, parents deserve all the help that can be provided. After all, their children are the future of our families and our country.

In the past, help for parents was usually readily available. For the most part, women did not work outside the home so mothers, grandmothers, aunts and other relatives were available to help. Neighbors relied on each other to watch children and community volunteers were called upon in times of crises. Today, many people don't know their next-door, neighbor; we see our neighbors only on garbage day. Statistically, our neighborhoods turn over at a rate of twenty percent per year.

So, who do parents turn to for help today? I would like to suggest that grandparents are part of the answer. Grandparents of today's young children are baby boomers, the generation born between the end of World War II and 1963. Boomers have had an impact upon American culture at every stage of their lives, and as they become grandparents they will change the face of grandparenting. Boomers are better educated, healthier, wealthier and are able to bring a broader range of experiences to grandparenting than any generation before them.

Grandmas have permission to spoil

As Allie passed the counter; she could see only one thing. It was a light tan beanie-baby puppy with large heavy front paws and a red heart around its left eye.

Allie fell in love with the puppy and knew she had to have it!

She told her Grandmother about it immediately. Grandma looked at the puppy and said, "It's cute, but we must get going." Allie was disappointed but knew there was still time.

Later that day, Allie and her Grandma walked by the cute little puppy and she said to her Grandmother, "Could I please get the puppy"?

Again, Grandma Laurie said, "We'll think about it." Allie knew this meant, "No!"

In the meantime, Allie went to see the dog and asked the salesperson to put it away, so no one else could buy it. She said, "Grandma, if you buy it, I will pay for it with my own money when I get home!"

At that moment, Grandma Laurie couldn't resist any longer. She reached into her coat pocket and pulled out the cute little puppy saying, "I was saving it for your birthday next week."

Allie, looked at the dog and said with a big smile said, "Thank you Grandma, you are so special!"

The analogy of "family" as a salad

Though the blood relation will remain at the core, a new family, a more diverse family structure has emerged. The term "salad" surfaced in research with the Grandparent Groups when they attempted to explain the diversity of family that is evident today in our society. Like it or not, the "salad" bowl of family is now a complex configuration of multiple marriages, single parents, multi-generational and ethnic families, single sex couples and blended families.

The traditional "family tree" no longer adequately depicts today's family. Every ingredient that goes into a salad changes the salad. The same holds true in today's family. Our families are taking on an entirely new configuration, more analogous to a salad than a tree. With the rise in divorces, interracial marriages, adoption, same sex parents, and single parents, today's family may bear little resemblance to the family of generations past. The "salad bowl" of family may or may not include any biological family, but rather may be made up of step-parents and grandparents, adopted parents, grandparents, aunts, uncles, brothers, sisters, neighbors and friends.

How has the family changed? The traditional family was made up of four grandparents; today's blended family may include six, eight or even ten sets of grandparents. The traditional family contained uncles and aunts but the blended family also includes friends and neighbors. The traditional family were blood relatives; today's family is much more apt to include blood relatives as well as neighbors and community.

Whatever the make-up or appearance of today's family, every child needs support. If the "salad" of family is what we create, what ingredient are you and what are you doing to sustain the values essential to family?

Grand-relations

I call the process of involving grandparents and great-grandparents in the family "Grand relations." The "Grand relations" network recognizes that parents need help. Grandparents serve as valuable mentors and play a critical role in children's lives. Because of the rapid evolution in the family structure over the past one hundred years, the entire process of creating "Grand-relations" within the families is changing. No family can "go it alone" for extended periods of time. Families need to find the resources for help and support that work for them.

Though we no longer live in an Ozzie and Harriet world, no one can deny the family's value and importance and to its children. Children need the comfort and security of family. Most grandparents want to be supportive but lack direction. Each blended family needs to find the recipe that works for them.

If you do not live near your biological family, it does not mean you can't be part of a family. Are you the neighborhood carpenter, hunter, gardener, math coach or chef? You could be the grandparent, uncle or aunt who lives far from your biological family and becomes part of your neighborhood family.

Get involved in building "Grand relations" in your family. You can make the difference that changes a life. Children are our most important assets and the ingredients of our future.

Ten absolutes of grandparenting

1. Support your grandchildren's dreams and love them unconditionally.
2. Treat your children and grandchildren with respect.
3. Communicate honestly and expect the same in return.
4. Participate in the lives of your grandchildren.
5. Know that it's what you do, not what you say, that counts most.
6. Let your grandchildren know who you are.
7. Be available to listen and listen carefully.
8. Be patient, let children be children.
9. Speak positively and support your grandchildrens' parents.
10. Live your life as an example for your children and grandchildren and tell them often that you love them.

Ideas & suggestions for parents

1. Family night

A family friend long ago developed a family night. They agreed to have one night together each week as a family. They arbitrarily chose Wednesday night to be their family night and a commitment was made by everyone. They have maintained their family night for over twenty-five years. Their agenda has completely changed, but one thing hasn't: they get together every Wednesday night no matter what. As the children have grown, left home and have had children, they still return each Wednesday night for family night with Grandma and Grandpa. Here are some of the guidelines they maintained over the years:

- Everyone participates and takes a turn at choosing what the activities will be
- Preparing the meal and cleaning up will be shared by everyone

2. Preparing to be a parent

Our lives change dramatically with the birth of our first child. Someone else suddenly becomes the focus. This change can be difficult if you are not fully prepared. I encourage you and your partner to discuss the following questions, record your responses and revaluate them often as your family matures:

- Am I mentally prepared for this new role?
- What are my new responsibilities as a parent?
- Why do I want to be a parent?
- Who will back me up and be my coach?
- What role will extended family play?
- What values do I want for my children to possess?
- Who is my parent role model?
- Do I want to parent the way I was parented? Why or why not?

Ideas & suggestions
for grandparents

1. Preparing to be a grandparent

It's time to take inventory of how you feel about be-coming a grandparent. Consider the following:

- How do you feel about being a grandparent?
- What is your personal relationship with both parents-to-be?
- Have you discussed with them how you want to be involved?
- How are you and your life different from that of your adult children?

2. Create your role

Communication will enhance your relationship today and in the future. Create a time for you and your adult children to discuss how you can best support them.

Talk with your adult child about your desire to spend time one-on-one with their children. If you want to help and be involved, you might consider asking the parents for their suggestions. Ingenuity and patience are required to create your new role.

4

Grandparenting 101

The day you became a grandparent

A relationship begins the day your grandchild is born. In fact, it might even begin before the child is born. Recently, I saw a picture of my future granddaughter four months before she was born. Some believe the grandparents should be there when the child is born. I believe grandparents should proceed cautiously here and honor the wishes of the parents.

Today it is possible to see your grandchild born when you are miles away using Internet technology. I spoke recently to a grandmother who witnessed the birth of her grandson in Florida while she was in New Jersey. She felt she was a part of this wonderful time, even though she was thousands of miles away.

It is important to get involved with your infant grandchild. This is true for grandfathers as well as grandmothers. Do not ignore these important and formative years. Many Boomer grandfathers helped raise their own children and possess a comfort level with young children. Early involvement will have long-term dividends.

Being an involved grandparent doesn't just happen with your new title. The foundation for a grandparent/grandchild relationship is established at infancy. As a grandparent, you are in a different place in life than you were as a parent. You've had practice, matured, grown in wisdom and understanding. You view the world differently now. You have so much to offer this new little person.

Enjoy this new chapter of your life. Trust that you have the tools and skills necessary to be a grandparent. Like parents, we become grandparents without a manual or road map. Believe that your life experiences and maturity have prepared you well for your new role.

Infant wisdom

Lilly was reading with her grandfather. Every now and then, she would reach up and touch her grandfather's wrinkly face and then touch her own.

As he was reading, she interrupted him and asked, "Grandpa, did God make you?" Grandpa replied, "Yes, He made me a long time ago." Then she said, "Grandpa, did God make me?"

Grandpa responded, "Yes, He did, not too long ago." Smiling as if a light had come on, she replied, "God's getting better, isn't He?"

Planning the grandparent role

Talk with your adult children about how they see your role as a grandparent. Remember at all times that the parents have the final say in what role you will play. Be open to discuss with the parents any of their thoughts and concerns.

A relationship with a grandchild will require your time and attention peppered with a lot of energy. One-on-one time with a grandchild is the catalyst for a special, rewarding life-long relationship.

Our precious grandchildren will have faults—look where they came from, but love them without conditions. This is the greatest gift you can give your grandchild.

The roles are different

Parent	Grandparent
Provide food, shelter, and clothing	A resource
Support child's performance	Support unconditionally
The front line member of the family	Important member of a larger family including great-grandparents, uncles, aunts, and cousins

Parent	Grandparent
Day-to-day life	Links to the past; including the parent's childhood and a broader perspective of family history
Makes the rules	Supports parental rules

Parents are in charge

As a grandparent you may feel that your adult children are too strict or too lenient as parents; you may be right. It doesn't matter. The parent is the parent and parents make the rules.

Yes, as a grandparent, you have experience with raising your children but your grandchildren are not your children. You raised your children and learned what works and doesn't. You now have a better idea of what's important and what's not. You have learned from your mistakes and want to keep your children from making the same mistakes. Don't do it.

Being critical of how your grandchildren are raised is the surest way to alienate your children and cause major rifts in family relationships. Grandparents must remember they are not in charge. Your role is one of support.

As parents, many grandparents dictated to their children when to pick up their crayons, where to hang their clothes, how to hold their pencils, when to apologize, when to take a break. Old parental habits must change in grandparenting.

Difficulties occur when grandparents fall back into the "old habits" of parenting. Parents set the standards for discipline and the grandparent must learn to accept this. Serious discipline or consequences are the parents' responsibility.

Those children we diapered and bandaged are now full-fledged adults who are making their own life decisions. Some of those decisions may be a direct contradiction to the decisions you would make. Remember to respect the parents' decisions. You do not have to agree but you must accept and respect.

"I hate my son-in-law and wish he would just leave. He will not allow me to see my grandson and I hate him for that."

This disagreement centered on religion. The grandmother told the child that his father's faith was strange and her religion made more sense. Grandmother refused to respect the beliefs of the parents. As a result of her disrespectful approach, she was the one left out. Four years later, the problem continues. The grandmother sees her grandson once a month. She still dislikes her son-in-law and they rarely speak. Her daughter too, has been affected and is staying away from her mother. She is caught in the middle and feels torn. Everyone loses: adult child, son in law, grandchild and grandparent.

Situations like this are not uncommon as our society becomes more and more diverse. This grandmother failed to recognize that parents are adults who will make decisions about their life and beliefs. Her attitude and unwillingness to accept and respect the wishes of the parent has created the problem and caused the family to grow apart.

Disagreements can occur in the areas of religion, politics, education, culture and discipline. Grandparents must understand they will never agree with their adult children on all aspects of child rearing. Grandparents need to be cautious even when their adult child specifically asks for input to not offer unsolicited advice and opinions. When a parent asks for help, help them by asking questions that will provide clarity.

"A grandparent provides support so the parents can find the solution."

Grandparent, be on guard and avoid judgments, no matter what has occurred. If the parent calls his or her spouse, "selfish and inconsiderate" and you agree, watch out. If there is a disagreement or argument between the parents, don't get involved. Comments made during volatile times can often come back to haunt you and have long-term negative consequences.

Parents and the grandparents must work to keep the lines of communication open. To reduce the anger when someone's feelings are hurt, use "I" statements. For example, "I'm hurt by what you said about my child." This encourages the conversation to move forward and minimize the anger.

If communication breaks down, agree to make the subject off limits temporarily, if not permanently. A statement such as, "I will no longer discuss my reasons for where Katie goes to school with you" ends the argument but keeps other lines of communication open. Communication between parents and grandparents must be clearly understood.

One common area for lack of understanding between parents and grandparents is the use of car seats. This is a challenging change for most grandparents. Studies show that many grandparents who do use car seats comply grudgingly. Care should be taken by the parents to show the grandparents how the car seat is installed and buckled. Grandparents need a little education to fully understand the safety value of car seats.

Breastfeeding is another area of misunderstanding. To nurse a child in a room full of people was unheard of a generation ago. Today this is common practice. Here again the rules have changed. The grandparent can choose to accept it or leave the room.

Daily activities should be discussed between parents and grandparents. Gifts, treats, the use of pacifiers, dolls and bedtimes are all areas that need to be mutually understood.

When grandparents determine what works with their grandchild, they can incorporate the material into their regular routine. Children love special books, songs and enjoy hearing stories about their parents when they were kids and grandparents want to find ways to help. These "gifts" of time and self provide a wonderful opportunity for grandparents to develop strong bonds with their grandchildren. These memories will far outlast the latest toy.

Grandpa Tom wanted to find a way to be helpful while visiting his grandchildren. He liked to sing and remembered a song he learned growing up. That night at bedtime he sang the song, from that night on, Grandpa was a hero. The grandchildren loved it and Grandpa discovered a gift that only he alone could provide. Not only did this give a nurturing exchange with his grandchildren but it rekindled a childhood memory that had long since been forgotten.

When your hat has two visors

Grandparents are often the parents' first call for help. When grandparents are called upon to care for their grandchildren, it's important to understand that your role has changed temporarily to that of primary caregiver. As the primary caregiver, the grandparent will be tested in new ways.

When we are asked to be the primary caregiver, the analogy of a "two-visor cap" may be helpful. Picture a cap with two visors, one with "parent" on the visor and the other "grandparent." When we fill in for the parents we assume the responsibility as the primary caregiver. Both you and your grandchild must understand that your responsibilities have changed. The two-visor cap is an effective way for you to remember that your duties have now become two-fold.

Last summer, Grandma Pat took her grandson, Charlie, to the lake for a week. As soon as they arrived, Pat took on her new role as the parent/grandparent. She knew her grandson had spent little time around water, so they immediately went for a hike around the cabin. Grandma answered many questions but also cautioned Charlie, as a mother or father would do, about areas around the cabin where he needed to be careful.

Charlie was surprised by the extra attention Grandma was giving, "I don't understand Grandma why you are telling me all this. I can take care of myself." Grandma Pat explained that she was not only his grandmother for the week but taking on the role of his mother and father. She told Charlie that she was doing things differently because her role was different. She also explained that she was responsible for his welfare and that she didn't want anything to happen to him. After the explanation, Charlie had a better understanding and accepted what his grandmother was doing.

Explain the change in your responsibilities to your grandchild. It will help you and also help the child to understand better why you seem different. The parent-grandparent, or care-giving grandparent, carries with it a more expansive slate of responsibilities and often these responsibilities are initially difficult for grandparents and grandchildren to understand and accept.

Grandpa Earl took care of his grandson Pete one afternoon when Pete's mother had a doctor appointment. They went into the backyard to swing and Pete fell and scratched his knee.

Earl could tell the wound wasn't serious, but knew he had to apply some first aid. It had been years since he had bandaged a scraped knee. He felt good when Pete showed his mom the evidence of his accident and said, "Grandpa Earl, helped me when I fell and gave me a treat when I stopped crying. I sure like my Grandpa."

Parents, prepare your own parents. Remember they are in the dark when it comes to the day-to-day care of your child. What are the rules, schedules, routines, habits, likes and dislikes of your child? What should grandma and grandpa expect? Remember, this little person is unique and it's been awhile since grandma and grandpa had this level of responsibility. Review this information with your children as well when they are old enough to understand.

It's the parent's responsibility to adequately inform the grandparents of safety requirements needed in the grandparent's home. Those so-called "little" pieces of information can be very valuable when small emergencies occur. Ruth Brown, in her book, *A Grandmother's Guide to Extended Babysitting*, reminds us how important it is to have everything clearly written down before the parents leave. Sometimes it's the little things, like which day the garbage man comes or the phone number of the veterinarian when the dog gets sick that makes it easier for the caregiver to do their job.

If we are not well prepared, the added responsibility as the primary caregiver can become an impossible and overwhelming task. Of course it's important to keep the child safe, but it's equally important not to lose perspective.

Parent-grandparents can have fun with their grandchildren. It's easy to be overprotective. Don't become too cautious and take away the opportunity for children to learn on their own, even from their mistakes.

"Grandparenting is serious business but should not be taken too seriously."

Grandparents might care for their grandchildren when the parents are out of town or at Grandma and Grandpa's house. Most grandparents notice a big difference in their grandchildren when the parents are not around. Some children do not react well to change and misbehave. Still others will "test" to see what they can get away with.

My grandchildren are usually on their best behavior when I'm visiting them in Sweden. My son and his wife often use this time for short "getaways." While they are gone, my granddaughters like to play games with me. I, of course, know only bits of Swedish while they are fluent in both Swedish and English. Language games provide a wonderful way for me to develop a relationship, learn a little more Swedish and have fun.

Often it's the simplest of actions that mean the most to a child.

"My grandfather became very sick and couldn't live by himself, so he came to live with us. Each morning, he would spend time with me before I would go to school. On weekends he taught me how to "carve." I remember this time with my grandfather as the best time of my life."

"When I was ten years old, my mother and father went on vacation and Grandma came to stay with me. Grandma wasn't fussy about many things, except making a bed. She would pull and pull to be sure the lines on the sheets were perfect and she taught me to do it the same way. Today, when I show my grandchildren how to make a bed, I tell them how I learned to make a bed."

Grandparents can provide meaningful breaks for parents

and be mentors at the same time. They've played this role since the beginning of time. Listening, having fun, telling stories, all the while paying close attention to safety are the valuable skills of an experienced grandparent.

Infant wisdom

Mark surprised his grandmother one morning by bringing her a cup of coffee. He had made it himself and was very proud. He waited anxiously to hear the verdict on the quality of the coffee. Grandmother had never had such a bad cup of coffee. As she forced down the last sip, she noticed three plastic figures in the bottom of her cup. She asked, "Honey, why are three of your little green army guys in the bottom of my cup?" Mark replied, "You know Grandma, it's like on TV, 'The best part of waking up is soldiers in your cup.'"

Ideas & suggestions
for parents

1. Conflict

If you are being defensive and you were in error, apologize and move on. Remember you are an adult; negotiate a solution. In a contest of wills, everyone looses:

- Do you have a strategy for dealing with family conflict?
- Are you being defensive about something you said or did in the past, or is this a new issue?
- Things are not always as they appear.
- Do you truly understand what the conflict is about or do you think you understand?
- Have you reached a verdict before you know the facts?
- Can you stay calm and allow yourself to be open-minded?
- Do you confirm that you understand by repeating back, before responding?

2. Correcting

Observe the number of times you correct your child. Each time you do, provide five positive statements of encouragement. You will be amazed how quickly your attitude and their behavior will change:

- Do you spend too much of your day correcting your children?
- Children should have choices and a clear understanding of the consequences of their behavior. Are you even aware you are being critical?
- What are you doing each day to encourage and stimulate your children?

Ideas & suggestions
for grandparents

1. Look at the world through a child's eyes

When you look at the world as a child, you will recall your interests as a child, and your role will be clear:

- What were three of your favorite things to do as a child?
- What do you remember doing with your own parents? Grandparents?
- Are you being observant?

If your grandchildren enjoy something you know little about, do your homework and learn all you can or ask them to teach you. Watch your grandchild, ask questions and observe what he or she likes to do. Let your grandchild take the lead.

2. My adult child thinks I'm interfering

If your child thinks you are interfering, you probably are, but don't quit there. Find out specifically how you are interfering and make efforts to change your behavior. Talk with your child and express your desire to assist, not control, the family environment.

Give yourself and your children time and be patient, with both of you.

Being together

5

Guiding the next generation

Discipline is not to be feared

Poor communication about discipline can easily result in family conflict. It is one of the primary reasons grandparents are reluctant to care for their grandchildren. They fear they won't know what to do when their grandchild misbehaves. "We were having such a great time at the zoo until my grandson decided he wanted another ice-cream cone. I didn't know what to do, so I took him home."

"Be creative and give yourself time."

Isn't it amazing how we shy away from things we are uncomfortable with? If you are uncomfortable taking care of your grandchildren, begin with one grandchild. Involve additional grandchildren, when you are comfortable handling the discipline issues and feel you have some control over the situation.

Grandma Anne enjoyed her one-on-one time with her grand-daughter until younger brother Jimmy was born. Jimmy just would not listen. This bothered Grandma Anne until she decided to have some one-on-one time with Jimmy. He was a different child. She couldn't believe the change. Soon she was comfortable handling both children.

Children will often "act out" when they think they are not getting enough attention. Feeling ignored, children will challenge you in immeasurable ways. Attention can be given positively or negatively. To be sure your grandchildren know what is expected, you may need to repeat the expectation.

Grandpa Bob was taking care of his grandson when his grandson said, "Grandpa, I want a cookie." Because it was almost dinnertime Grandpa said, "I understand you want a cookie but you will have to wait until after dinner." His grandson didn't like Grandpa's answer, but knew he had been heard.

Positive discipline: catch the child being good

When I was teaching, I often used a game called, "Catch the child being good." Each day, I would single out two children and write positive notes the children would take home to their parents. In the notes, I would explain specifically why the child had merited recognition. "I really appreciated how well you cleaned your workspace before lunch. Thank you!"

This same method can work for parents and grandparents. When children know they are rewarded for positive behavior, they will expend less energy misbehaving and more energy finding ways to gain positive recognition. Parents and children love it.

Grandparents can do the same thing. Tell your grandchild you intend to reward him or her for a particular good behavior today and that you will write a note to mom and dad telling them all about it.

Dear Mom and Dad,

Peter was a very big help today at Grandma's house. He helped me pull two buckets of weeds and never complained. The garden looks beautiful. We had fun working together. I am so proud of what a good worker Peter is and I love it when he comes.

Grandma Juju

Reward charts

Your grandchildren will work hard if they clearly understand what is expected. If a child does something wrong, give the misbehavior minimal attention. When the child does something correctly, praise, praise, and praise again. Give praise to the child, praise to the parent and praise to the child again in the presence of the parents.

A tool often used to support a particular change of behavior is a reward chart. Reward charts work effectively for most children ages three and older. The primary objective is to give attention to the positive behavior and slowly the negative behavior will diminish. The premise is: if you concentrate on and reward positive behavior, you will get positive results.

The key to making reward charts work effectively is to keep the behavior and the reward fresh in the child's mind. The process of creating a reward chart can be as simple as writing the desired behavior and the reward on a piece of paper. Stickers, stars or happy faces are great for rewards.

Develop the chart with the involvement of the child, the parents and the grandparents:

- Get "buy-in" from all parties.
- Be sure the child understands clearly what is expected.
- Reward the appropriate behavior immediately.
- Reward often, especially in the beginning, to create a positive behavior pattern.
- Use the chart for one or two behaviors at a time.
- Be a bit more lenient at the beginning, slowly raising the standards once the behavior becomes habitual.
- If the program isn't working, consider lowering the expectations until everyone has positive results.
- Make changes often.
- If more than one child is participating, your task is to make sure everyone is successful.
- Be consistent! The primary reason for failure is usually the parent or grandparent. Follow-through is the key to making the chart work effectively.
- Place the chart in a prominent position so it won't be overlooked. The refrigerator is often used for posting the chart.
- Finally, make the chart fun for everyone. Encourage, praise and reward.

A grandfather once told me that charts didn't work for his grandson. After two days, the child no longer paid any attention to the chart. This is not a failure, but a success. If the chart works for two days, make the necessary changes and continue. Be sure you are doing all you are doing to make the chart a success.

With small changes, the game starts again. With each effort, the child learns, is rewarded and grows.

Enjoy your grandchildren more

1. **Boundaries are necessary for control and safety**
   Once an activity actually starts, it's too late. Being clear about expectations before the activity will help the child understand his or her boundaries. Boundaries free you and the child to enjoy the activity more fully.

2. **Use "I" statements**
   "I" statements are simple expressions designed to end differences of opinion between you and your grandchild. "I" statements can be used for positive as well as negative behavior. Make "I" statements a part of your normal dealings with children.
   "It makes me very sad when I see you hit your brother . . . "
   "I am unhappy when I see you are not listening to me . . . "
   "I really like it when you hug your sister . . . "

3. **Look at the person who is speaking**
   Physical distance between you and the child when you are talking makes a difference in the child's ability to pay attention. Whenever you are trying to make a point, physically get the child close to you and have them look into your eyes.

4. **Plan all activities carefully**
   Discuss with the child what he or she would like to do. Give careful thought to the age appropriateness of the activities before you begin. This is not to say you can't do things compulsively but it's often better to have a plan. Giving children choices will increase their self-love.

5. **Spend time alone with each grandchild**

   When possible, work with one grandchild at a time. Many grandparents find it difficult to work with more than one grandchild at a time. This is not unusual and nothing to be ashamed of. We all know how good it feels to have someone important give his or her undivided attention.

6. **Allow time to ask questions**

   The surest way to know if a grandchild understands is to ask questions. Everything may be clear to you but it's more important that it is also clear to your grandchild.

7. **Avoid showing favoritism**

   Grandfathers can relate to girls as well as boys. Children enjoy spending time with both grandparents.

8. **All rules need to be consistent with parents' wishes**

   Remember to support the parents and the entire activity will go much smoother. Don't be afraid to restate the rules as many times as necessary. Writing the rules and posting them or bringing them along is a good idea. If a rule is violated during the activity, ask the child to read the rules again.

9. **Have fun!**

   There is no substitute for good old-fashioned belly laughs. It's good for you, your grandchild and your relationship. Share with your grandchild how excited you are about being with them.

   Parents enjoy the break. Children enjoy getting away from their parents for short periods of time and Grandparents enjoy being part of a very important relationship.

Grandma and Grandpa's house

Grandparents have every right to make the rules in their own homes but remember to be reasonable and focus on what is really important. Any rule that is different from home should be discussed with the parents and grandchildren. Expecting grandchildren to wash their hands before meals is a reasonable expectation even if it's not stringently followed at home.

Children should not be asked to keep secrets about rules. So-called "secrets" breach trust between parents and grandparents. When the child is under your supervision, your number one rule remains: "support the wishes of the parent."

Open and frequent communication with the parents and the grandchild is critical:

- Write out the important rules and identify the consequences if the rules are not adhered to.
- Follow the parents' rules consistently.
- Provide rewards or acknowledgement when the rules are followed.
- When rules are not followed, consequences must be immediate and consistent.
- Reinforce the rules on an "as needed" basis.
- Be sure the child fully understands each rule they are expected to adhere to.
- At all times, be realistic; remember you are working with a child.

Bullying

Bullying is the ultimate form of disrespect and is extremely harmful to a child's self-concept. Fortunately, parents and grandparents can do much to help children who are the subjects of bullying.

We bully others simply because we do not feel someone has

Infant wisdom

As Grandpa Floyd and family were getting ready to drive to Grandparent Camp, Grandpa reviewed the rules for the trip.

He said, "If anyone wants to go to the bathroom, hold up two fingers!"

Grandson Hunter quickly asked, "How will that help?"

equal value. The most common reasons for bullying are: different skin color, speech, beliefs, status, appearance, hair and clothing. According to Barbara Coloroso, a leading expert and author on bullying, "Bullying is a conscious, willful and deliberate hostile activity intended to instill harm." Barbara also states that over 160,000 students miss school each day because of bullying.

Adults contribute to the problem when they ignore what is happening. "Boys will be boys" is not an excuse for bullying. Be aware; girls can also be bullies.

Children who are shown empathy and are encouraged to display a caring respectful attitude, will refuse to take part in bullying activities. Children possess a natural caring and respectful attitude at a very young age. I witnessed this recently when my newest granddaughter was born. My son's friends brought their six-month-old Jon to the hospital to see my granddaughter. While visiting, my two-day-old granddaughter started to cry. As soon as she started to cry, the six-month-old little boy began to cry as well. The next time you're in a restaurant and a young child is crying, look around. Many of the other children will be trying to see what's wrong; they have looks of concern and want to help.

Teaching children at a young age that they are capable of making good choices will help provide the child with the necessary self-concept to withstand bullying. Children will find comfort in their choices and tend not to follow the example of a bully.

Parents can help their child by providing opportunities for them to make simple choices. At bedtime, give a two-year-old the choice between red and blue pajamas. At age three, we might say, "I laid out three dresses. You decide which one you would like to wear." At age five, we might say, "We are going to church soon, please get dressed." Giving choices will teach the child to own the consequences of their own actions.

Grandparents can help by providing choices as well. "I'm coming over to take you out to breakfast. Would you like to go to Perkins or Denny's?" A relatively easy choice when the child objects to getting into the car seat could be, "Get in or stay home." If the child makes a bad choice, you need to live with it and support it. Providing simple choices will help children later when they need to make choices of greater consequence.

Laughing at someone instead of with them can cause great pain if it's done at the expense of a vulnerable child. Making fun of others is a tactic used for control and regularly used by gangs. Parents and grandparents can help children by helping children to recognize bullying and sharing some of your own experiences:

One grandfather shared the following story with his grandson. "I experienced bullying when I was your age. I had fallen down the steps at school and three girls made fun of me and called me names. The fall hurt, but the laughing hurt more. I tried to ignore them but the hurt and embarrassment lasted longer than the pain from my knee."

Some children have difficulty recognizing when they are being bullied. They may think it's just teasing.

"My granddaughter tried out for cheerleading recently. When she didn't make the squad the cheerleaders wouldn't sit with her at lunch. When she tried to join them at their table, they all got up and left."

A good rule is, if the laughter hurts, it has gone too far. It's time to quit and an apology is in order.

What parents & grandparents can do to prevent bullying

- Recognize bullying as real and painful.
- Realize that bullying can be practiced by young and old.
- Teach children to develop friendships. Friendships provide positive examples.
- Create opportunities for children to get involved in energizing activities with children from other backgrounds.
- Teach children about choices when they are young.
- Provide a simple reason for every rule.
- Closely monitor television, videogame and computer use.
- Teach children empathy and model it yourself.

Five tips to improve communication with your grandchildren

1. Talk to your grandchildren in words they understand
2. Physically get close and look them in the eyes when you are talking
3. Let your grandchildren ask questions.

4. Listen to their responses and be prepared, your grandchildren may not always agree
5. Set the ground rules before you begin an activity together

Favoritism

To not show favoritism can be a challenge for parents and grandparents. Webster defines favoritism as "The disposition to favor and promote the interest of one person or family to the neglect of others."

Human nature draws us to one child over another. We all need to be reminded that all children need your love. Sometimes, favoritism can occur along the lines of gender: father with son, grandmothers with granddaughters and grandfathers with grandsons.

Grandpa Jim chose to play with his grandsons but never his granddaughters. One day, his granddaughter Sharon complained to Grandma, "How come I never get to spend any fun time with Grandpa? He never plays with me. He always has time for my brothers."

Grandpa Jim overheard Sharon's conversation and recognized that indeed she was right; he spent lots of time with his grandson's but never with Sharon. Right then and there Grandpa Jim made up his mind to do something special with Sharon.

The next weekend, when he arrived at Sharon's house he proudly announced, "Today is Granddaughter Day." He had prepared a list of activities that they could do that day. Sharon chose a trip to the mall. When she returned, the big smile on Sharon's face told the rest of the story.

Most favoritism is unconscious. A simple test to determine if you are guilty of favoritism is to question someone close to you. Chances are their response will be unbiased. If you are guilty; make a conscious decision to change.

Grandma Betty was cooking in the kitchen when her grand-daughter and grandson Joey stopped by. She asked her grand-daughter if she would like to help her make cookies and suggested Joey to his grandfather mow the grass.

A few minutes later, Joey came back in the house and said, "I don't want to mow grass, but I would like to help bake cookies with you.

Grandma Betty thought for a moment and said, "Why not, there is no reason you can't help make cookies."

Many years later, Joe, as he now wants to be called, has completed training to be a chef and will be starting his first job."

Grandma Betty learned two important lessons: Listen to the interests of your grandchildren and then help them follow their dreams and never, let gender get in your way.

Infant wisdom

One afternoon, my grandson was playing with Oreo, my dog, when he suddenly blurted out, "Your dog has bad breath!"

He promptly marched into the bathroom and came out with a bottle of Listerine and proceeded to pour a goodly amount into Oreo's water dish.

I asked him what he thought he was doing. His reply was, "Whenever Daddy has bad breath, Mommy gives him Listerine."

What's nature anyway?

Grandpa Rick and his, six-year-old grandson, Jimmy were canoeing on Lake Wapogasset. It was an absolutely perfect day; the water was still, the sun was shining and the temperature was around sixty degrees.

As they canoed quietly across the lake, they spotted a Great Blue Heron standing near the cattails. Jimmy watched carefully, he had never seen a heron before. They paddled closer and when they were a short distance away, the bird vaulted into the air and majestically flew only a few feet above Jimmy's head. As the bird flew over their canoe, a few drops of water fell on Jimmy. There was a long silence when neither said a word and finally Jimmy said, "Wow, isn't nature wonderful?"

Grandpa Rick was proud and glowing inside, for providing this wonderful opportunity to observe nature at its best to his grandson.

I ran into Rick and Jimmy later that day, still talking and excited about their experience. I commented to Grandpa Rick about how much I believe Jimmy learned that morning about nature.

He started to laugh and told me the rest of the story; as soon as they were back on shore, Jimmy turned to his Grandpa and asked, "What is nature anyway?"

Grandpa Rick and Jimmy have a shared experience and a great story to tell for years to come.

Ideas & suggestions
for parents

1. What do you do about favoritism?

It's difficult for parents to treat each child the same. This situation can be especially difficult if one child demands more attention than another. We were all born as unique individuals; thank God! We also know that some children are easier to be around than others.

Situations such as illness force us to temporarily give additional attention to one child over another. When this happens, our parental abilities are taxed to the limit. It's important to remember that this situation will pass and when it does, you will be in a position to provide attention to the other children.

When things are temporarily out of balance, talk to the other children, tell them that you love them and explain why things will be different for a short time. This is especially true with younger children who can't understand on their own.

Ideas & suggestions
for grandparents

1. Boundaries

Establishing boundaries or rules are not the hard part; enforcing them is. The following are examples of some simple boundaries when going on an outing with a young grandchild:

- When I call your name, answer me right away.
- We will stay together and not go off on our own.
- When I say it's time to go home, there will be no complaining.
- Always ask the child, "Do you understand?" Wait for an affirmative response.

2. Provide a break for parents

Parents get overwhelmed, tired and need a break from their children. An unscheduled break for your adult child can be a real treat. If you live close, you have a real advantage; drop by and take the children to the park. If you are at a distance, schedule a time when you can provide parents a break and don't forget to enjoy your grandchildren in the process.

Generations learning together and from each other

6

Not all grandparents are the same

Been there—When asked—Forever

Through research, conversations and observations I have concluded there are three types of grandparents, the "Been There, Done That," the "Help When Asked," and the "Parents Forever." Each group has a distinctive set of characteristics and sees their roll as grandparent quite differently. Most grandparents feel their primary role is to be a resource to the parents, to love, support and listen.

Approximately one-third of all grandparents belong to each group at any particular time; the groups are dynamic and ever changing. Many reasons contribute to these changes: physical distance between families, illness, jobs, disagreements or simply the decision to change.

In general, younger grandparents tend to belong to The "Parents Forever" group. An increasing number of grandparents, regardless of their ages, with grandchildren under five years of age, tend to be "Parents Forever." As grandparents age and have additional grandchildren, grandparents tend to become less involved and become the "Been There, Done That" grandparents. Grandma and Grandpa may not necessarily be in the same group at the same time. Grandma can be very involved while Grandpa takes a more passive role.

For the most part, men tend to follow the lead of their spouse and are more apt to be in the category of "Help When Asked." The "Been There, Done That" grandparents tend to be older grandparents or great-grandparents.

A word of caution: Some people should not be encouraged to be around our children. People who have been abused or demonstrate deviant behaviors need professional help. Until they receive such help, parents, grandparents and extended family should be on guard.

The "Been There, Done That" grandparents

Usually the "Been There, Done That" grandparents come from large families and have raised large families. Their attitude is; "enough is enough." In their minds', they have met society's expectations and need a rest. Some parents believe that once their children are grown, they are finished with any active involvement with the next generation.

The "Been There, Done That" grandparents believe it's up to the next generation to raise the children.

"I'm a seventy-year-old grandmother, I'm getting too old to crawl around on the floor with a two-year-old. I let the younger ones do that. I send them a little money each year for their birthday and that's the extent of my involvement."

A grandfather agreed, "I do a lot for my grandchildren. When they are born, I give each of them $100.00 and then each year for their birthday they get $10.00. I think I do a lot!"

The "Been There, Done That" grandparents are unwilling to provide the time and the effort necessary to stay connected. They often use the rationale, "My grandchildren are too busy. They never come to see us, so why should I go see them? As they grew, I tried to show my interest by attending their events, but they never seemed to care whether I was there or not."

One grandmother regrets that she didn't choose to be involved as a grandparent earlier. "When I was younger and my grand-children were young, I was just too busy to be involved with my grandchildren. Now that I have retired and have more time, they don't have time for me. I guess I got what I sowed."

Often "Been There, Done That" grandparents would rather buy the child something rather than give of their time. Many too, would rather tell you about their aches and pains than listen to their children or grandchildren.

The "Help When Asked" grandparents

The "Help When Asked" grandparents take a middle-of-the-road approach, willing to help, but only when asked to do so, by their children or grandchildren:

- They enjoy their own lives and fear it would change if they became involved with their grandchildren.
- They often do not have a good relationship with their adult child or their spouse.
- They understand some need for involvement but believe they have done their part.
- The help they provide is over and above what they perceive as their "responsibility."
- They are concerned that their involvement will be perceived as interference.

The "Help When Asked" grandparents tend to believe that if you're not sure how to help, you are better off not being involved. When the parents ask for help, their role is clearer and they feel they are no longer interfering.

This group of grandparents is typically made up of "take charge" personalities. Playing a supportive role is something they are unaccustomed to. Many grandfathers take this stand and leave the responsibility to the grandmothers. Some of the "Help When Asked" grandparents are modeling the example of their own parents who took a similar approach. They lacked effective mentors in their own lives and now their fears and insecurities keep them away.

In general, the "Help When Asked" grandparents believe that the parents are doing a better job than they did as parents.

"It's the parent's job and they are doing a better job than I did, I will help only when asked."

"I had six children and now have eleven grandchildren. The children range in age from one to twenty-three. I never had the education that my children had and they do a much better job than I can."

Some grandparents feel that the world has changed too much; parenting requires skills they don't have or today's children are too difficult to understand and relate to and they can't deal with the changes. When life circumstances change, through death or divorce, some single grandparents are no longer comfortable with the responsibility of caring for grandchildren.

"The way my son raises his children is much different than we raised our children. When the children don't behave, he talks to them. I'm not good at that."

"Help When Asked" grandparents often come from large families and are tired of having children around. They were still raising their own children when their first grandchildren were born.

Many "Help When Asked" grandparents work outside the home, have less time for grandchildren and are less willing to help parents. As grandchildren move further away, grandparenting activities are reduced.

If the grandparents have a large number of grandchildren, rather than risk showing favoritism, they choose to not get involved unless asked. The mere thought of being involved in the lives of numerous grandchildren is overwhelming to them.

"I have four beautiful grandchildren. I help when I can but it's hard to take care of all of them at the same time. I help when my daughter calls. She's a real good mother."

Parents should recognize that if their parents are "Help When Asked," they are not going to offer to help unless they are asked. They will help but only when asked. It's important for parents to ask the grandparents for help when needed. Ask the grandparents to be responsible for one child at a time. Chances are they are just waiting to be asked.

The "Parents Forever" grandparents

"Parents Forever" grandparents believe the old adage, "Once a parent, always a parent." The "Parents Forever" grandparent represents approximately 50% of all boomer grandparents but only 33% of the overall grandparent population today. Many of the grandfathers as well as the grandmothers are involved in the day-to-day care of their grandchildren.

The "Parents Forever" grandparents often say privately, "I never did enough for my children; I was always too busy and I want to do more now that I have time. I want to help my children and grandchildren in any way I can."

Another way to describe "Parents Forever" is with the word: "action." These grandparents are involved in the daily lives of their grandchildren. They have found that their involvement reinforces the important relationship with their grandchild and keeps them connected to the lives of their adult children. "Parents Forever" believe in the "It takes a village" philosophy of raising grandchildren. They see their role in the family as second only to the parents.

> *"I will never forget what my grandfather and grandmother did for me. When my parents got a divorce, I went to their home and stayed for over a month. They were the ones who explained to me that my parents were getting a divorce and what it meant. They told me that no matter what would happen with my mom and dad, they would be there for me as long as I lived, and they were. My grandparents had a lasting effect on my life. My grandfather taught me my love of music and my grandmother taught me to have faith. I owe a great deal to both of them and today I want to give to my grandchildren some of what I received from my grandparents."*

Many of the "Parents Forever" grandparents had one or more wonderful mentors who had a significant impact on their lives. They experienced the love, support and wisdom of their parents and grandparents and want to pass this on to their own grandchildren.

"Grandparents Forever" are highly motivated to nurture and protect their grandchildren. For them, family provides needed respite from the harshness of today's world, the tragedies, violence and terrorism. They want their grandchildren to feel loved, secure and protected.

They enjoy the "action" and the opportunity to participate in new adventures, especially when those activities allow them to share their experience or expertise. They value education and relish any experience that provides exposure to new things.

A prediction

Though it's too early to be certain, research leads me to believe we are on the cusp of a great change, a change in which grandparents will choose to "take action" and get involved in their grandchildren's lives. This comes at a time when grandchildren need our involvement more than any previous generation.

Cataclysmic world events, an increase in terrorism, the use of illegal drugs, alcoholism, gambling, divorce and crime will continue to reinforce the importance of grandparent's involvement.

Infant wisdom

As grandpa and his six-year-old granddaughter were driving home from Grandparent Camp, Grandpa Dick asked his granddaughter what she liked about camp. Sadie replied, "I liked when we got to look into the telescope at the lake." Grandpa asked, "What did you see?"

Sadie replied, "The lake was covered with *allergy* . . . I guess that's why we couldn't go swimming."

Ideas & suggestions
for parents

1. My parents won't help

If your parents won't help, accept it and remember it the day you become a grandparent. Some grandparents don't, or won't, ever believe they have any responsibility for their grandchildren. Find someone else. The village is full of grandparents.

There are adults other than your parents who are willing to take on the grandparent role for your children. Shirley had a brother who assumed the role of grandparent and took her son, Chris with him everywhere. When the grandparents saw the relationship Jim had with their grandson, they realized what they were missing. Many aunts and uncles assume the role of grandparents, especially when there is distance or medical restrictions.

This is a wonderful way for children to develop close relationships with numerous family members.

2. My parents won't follow my rules

You are the boss where your children are concerned. Set limits you can live with and enforce them when necessary. Communicate your rules clearly to the grandparents. Explain that it is not necessary that they agree with your rules but they must agree to abide by them. Ask the grandparents specifically if they can respect your rules and request an answer. This is your right.

New information about raising children is available today that wasn't available to your parents. Sharing this information will go a long way to gaining grandparents' support.

If necessary, reinforce your agreement by giving the grandparents a written copy of the rules.

3. My parents are not comfortable

Your parents' age and their health, as well as the age of your children and their energy level must be considered when you leave your children with their grandparents. If your parents are nervous around a toddler, it may be because they're concerned they won't be able to adequately supervise the child. Your child's safety is paramount, so take their concerns seriously. Keep visits short and be around for back up until you're confident your children will be safe. Create opportunities for them to spend time one-on-one with your children. Encourage their involvement in your planning. Experience and a better understanding of what to expect will quickly increase their comfort level.

Don't be offended; your parents' discomfort around your child is often their insecurity and not your child's behavior.

Men especially seem to be more comfortable with older children than with babies or toddlers and a three-year-old's incessant questions can sometimes try the nerves of the most patient individual.

Some grandparents are more comfortable around older children and can be wonderful mentors to teenagers, so don't "write them off."

**Ideas & suggestions
for grandparents**

1. **What type of grandparent are you?**

    "Been There, Done That,"

    "Help When Asked" or

    "Parents Forever"?

Many of us learned our approach to grandparenting from our own parents and grandparents, but that
doesn't explain why we think the way we do today. Where
do your feelings about grandparenting come from?

All three types of grandparents may be represented in
any given family. Examine the makeup of your family.

- How would you characterize your mother, father,
  and maternal and paternal grandparents?
- How do you remember your grandparents?
- What do you remember your parents saying
  about your grandparents?
- Describe yourself as a grandparent. Are you the
  grandparent you want to be?
- What kind of grandparent would you like to be?

2. Communicating about feelings

Dealing with feelings at a prime age provides children
with the experience necessary to be an emotionally
healthy adult. When we share our true feelings we provide an opportunity for our children and grandchildren to see who we really are. True feelings open the
door for our children to better understand, accept
and appreciate us. For too long, men particularly were
taught not to cry, get upset or express feelings. When

your grandchildren witness you being honest and open with them, they are more likely to feel comfortable sharing their true feelings with you.

Encourage your grandchildren to express their feelings. It gives them freedom and a valuable life skill.

- Are you open to sharing your feelings with your grandchildren?
- How well do you deal with strong feelings?
- Are you uncomfortable letting your children and grandchildren know when your feelings have been hurt?
- What do you say when your child or grandchild hurts your feelings?

3. Dealing with tragedy

Sooner or later tragedy occurs in everyone's life. It's a part of life that no one escapes. When tragedy occurs, what do you do?

Perhaps your child or grandchild is ill or your spouse dies unexpectedly. Sharing our pain can provide comfort we never thought possible. Involve your extended family and encourage their help and support.

How you handle tragedy will be a model for your children and your grandchildren.

4. My grandchild has special needs

Children with special needs require more time and special training. The child's needs may be emotional, physical or educational. It is important to know how you feel about working with this special child. If you feel angry or helpless, know that these feelings are normal.

There are many resources available to help your grandchild. If your grandchild has been diagnosed with attention deficit disorder (ADD) or a similar learning disability, the following are only a few of the resources available to you, your child and grandchild.

Learning Disabilities Association of America
www.ldanatl.org

The International Dyslexia Association
www.interdys.org

The National Center for Learning Disabilities
www.ncld.org

Schwab Foundation for Learning
www.schwablearning.org

Attention Deficit Disorder Association
www.adda.org

Children and Adults with Attention Deficit Disorders
www.chadd.org

Similar organizations are available in the United States for virtually all special needs, disorders and illnesses.

Whatever the disability, I urge you to learn all you can about your grandchild's uniqueness and accept his or her special needs as an added opportunity for your involvement.

7

A look at yourself

We are the mirror image

Our parents, our adult children and our grandchildren can teach us about ourselves. I call it the "Two-Way Reflection of Life."

When we are young, we watch our parents and made child-like evaluations of what we observe. We imitated what we saw and hear without judgments. By watching others, we acquire basic knowledge. How many times have you seen little girls putting on makeup and little boys shaving long before their first hint of a beard?

What we are exposed to affects our perception of the world. A recent newspaper story told of a young girl confined to a dark room and given very little food or human contact for the first several years of her life. Shortly after she was discovered, she was adopted. Since she had never been given guidance and reacted to being deprived, she would raid the refrigerator and became sick from overeating. Her adopted parents were forced to put a lock on the refrigerator door to curtail her eating. Gradually she learned how to eat by emulating her parents and the locks were removed.

Hopefully, most adults will have a positive influence on children, but not always. Children will quickly mirror things we don't want them to imitate. Some common examples are; smoking, drinking, swearing and poor grammar.

Not too long ago I observed my father touching his nose before he spoke. Usually this means he is somewhat uncomfortable about what he is about to say. Later, I viewed a video of one of my presentations and witnessed myself doing the very same thing. I had been nervous and reacted with the same unconscious gesture.

The three-way reflection of life

As we grow into adulthood, the mirror reflection of life evolves and other facets emerge through education, observation, experience and wisdom. This newly expanded mirror provides a clearer picture of who we really are. We can no longer blame others for what we have become. Parenting and Grandparenting can provide us with an opportunity to change what we don't like and reinforce those values and behaviors we hold strong. This "three-way reflection" helps us see the positive and negative behaviors we've contributed to in others.

The process of looking into the three-way mirror continues throughout our lives. We spend the first years emulating others, then screening out and reinforcing what we like or dislike. Sometimes, when we spend time with our family and friends, we unconsciously see ourselves.

I enjoy spending time with my sons and granddaughters and hearing about their successes. When they experience success, I silently take part ownership. We owe it to ourselves to acknowledge our part in our family's accomplishments. Look into the reflective mirror and reward yourself for your children and grandchildren's achievements. Within your heart you know that some of their decisions have been affected by your positive influence. Ultimately, your child made the final choice and your role is to be witness to their success. Graduations, awards, weddings and new babies are all occasions for parents and grandparents to reflect with pride on the role they played.

"Don't overlook this opportunity to experience your accomplishments."

Parents often say their greatest accomplishment in life was raising their children. One reason they feel that way is that it reinforces their contribution to making the world a better place.

The reverse is also true. When our children and grandchildren experience failure, we should be careful not to take on their responsibility. We cannot change the past; we can learn from it and shape our future. Give your children the freedom to make choices. They have the right to learn from experience. We can guide and support but never control.

This "three-way reflection" provides us the opportunity to see more clearly who we are. We now have wisdom and experience to determine who we want to be. If your father was a cold-hearted, uncaring person, you can choose to be a warm-hearted, caring person. Fortunately, adults can choose to discard what we want to reflect and become the person we choose to be.

The "three-way reflection" provides a clearer perspective of what we want our grandchildren to reflect. Observe the behavior of your children and grandchildren:

- How do they live their lives?
- What is their attitude toward life?
- How do they interact within the family and with others?

- What are their interests?
- What do they have a passion for?
- Are they constantly trying to prove something? Is there self-acceptance?
- Are your children living the life you would want for them?
- Is what you observe a reflection of your own life?

Do you see yourself in your grandchildren?

Our grandchildren acquire not only their parents' traits but also the traits of other adults, including their grandparents. We can hope these behaviors are positive.

When I drink my coffee, I have a tendency to slurp. The last time we visited, I was sitting with my granddaughter having a cup of coffee. I turned and looked when I heard her slurp her drink in exactly the same way. I was amused and astonished at the same time. Did I really make that much noise? I couldn't help but be a little embarrassed about my habit over the years. Suffice it to say, I have been trying to drink quietly ever since.

I'm inclined to get carried away joking with my grandchildren. I think I'm being funny, but sometimes I inadvertently hurt their feelings. On one occasion, I observed my grandchild doing the same thing, hurting her sister in the process. Suddenly, I became more aware of the consequences of my actions. Now it's up to me to modify my behavior.

Knowing and owning who we are can provide a new impetus for change. With this clearer picture of our true self, we can consciously choose and mirror who we want to be.

Mentor

A thirty-four year old granddaughter wrote the following letter to her dying Grandfather.

Dear Grandpa,

It's 5:00 A.M. and my internal clock must be preparing me for my third baby. I'm ready and waiting with great anticipation for this new little one to arrive.

At the same time, you have been on my mind daily. Grandpa: I'm so sorry you are sick. I wish I could be there to take away your discomfort, to support you and help in any way possible. Because I can't be there in person, I thought I would write this note.

You are an incredible person and have made a lifelong impact on my life as a Grandpa and a role model.

As I sit here thinking of you, I recall some of my fondest memories. I remember the trips you and Grandma made to visit us, Christmas with Santa, the ski trips to the mountains, the Easter egg hunts, the special trips I took to visit you and Grandma on the bus, our priceless time at the lake and all our wonderful meals and family gatherings.

You created lifelong memories and tradition that will live forever. You always made me feel so welcome and so loved! I only hope my children's grandparents will make an impact and be there, as you have been for me.

I'm sure it can't be easy for you Grandpa. Each day may seem like a struggle. Know that the people who love you the most are here to give back only a small piece of what you have given to them.

I love you, Grandpa!

M

Don't wait to thank people who have been important in your life. How many times have you heard someone say? "I wish my father and mother were still alive, so I could tell them how much I appreciate what they did for me."

Mentors inspire

Grandparent mentors helped shape the lives of the following successful Americans:

Olympians Jack, Jim and Jim Shea

One month before the opening of the 2002 Olympic games in Salt Lake City, Grandpa Jack Shea carried the Olympic Torch to light the cauldron. His son, Jim Shea was about to become the world's first third-generation Olympian. Grandfather Shea had won the gold medal in speed skating in the 1932 Olympics in his hometown of Lake Placid at the age of 22. His son, Jim, competed in the 1964 Olympics as a Nordic skier in Innsbruck, Austria. Jack's grandson, Jim, won the gold in the Skeleton event in Salt Lake City in 2002. Unfortunately, Grandpa Jack died in a car accident just one month before the start of the Olympics in which his grandson won the gold medal.

Astronaut Duane Cary

St. Paul, Minnesota native Duane Carey took only one personal treasure with him aboard the spaceship Columbia in July 2002. It was a Swiss army knife that his grandmother had given to him when he was eleven. When the astronaut was asked why, he replied, "Her dream was to see me blast off."

Pilots Charles and Eric Lindbergh

On May 21, 2002, exactly seventy-five years after Charles Lindbergh completed his historical Trans-Atlantic flight, grandson Erik took off to replicate his grandfather's flight. "I've dreamed for years of flying across the Atlantic," Erik stated to reporters before he took off for Paris. "My journey is a celebration of my grandfather's achievement."

In my research with the grandparent and parent groups, mentoring was often mentioned as one of the most important roles of a grandparents. A mentor willingly shares, teaches, supports, inspires and provides direction for another person. Parents and grandparents can be mentors in many ways.

Susan believed in supporting her community. She volunteered at the local Red Cross once a month to assist with blood donations. Her granddaughter later became her helper.

Mike and Martha always said a prayer before their evening meal. Before they ate, they encouraged everyone to share a memory that made their day special.

Jim's passion was reading. Once a month, he volunteered in his grandson's reading program. In the first grade program, Jim helped as an adult listener. It was a big deal for Andy when Grandpa came with him to school.

Mentors are an example to those who are willing to listen or observe. In mentoring, the example is provided, and then it's up to the observer what they will do with it. We can only hope that the example is respected and potentially assimilated but we may never know the final result.

Many years ago, I hired a manager for our business. I groomed him and taught him the "ins and outs" of the business. I felt good about our relationship and was disappointed the day he decided to leave.

Some years later, we had an occasion to talk. He told me that he saw me as a father figure and that I had done much to teach him valuable skills that he has applied to his work as well as his personal life. He thanked me for mentoring him and helping him to find direction in his life.

Today, he is married with two children and vice president of a large company,

It made my day to know that I had a positive impact on another human being's life. Often the example shared not only helps those intended, but many others. As a result, I decided to look at the people in my life who had influenced me and to let them know how much I appreciate what they had given me.

The best thank you

Dapper Dan was the nickname I bestowed on the most difficult child I ever taught. Unfortunately, Dan represents many children and grandchildren who are begging for our love.

Dan looked to me as a father/teacher. Unfortunately, he received little love and attention from his mother and father. Fortunately, Dan had a caring grandmother. She was elderly, not very strong and couldn't keep up with the busy first grader but knew how to give herself to Dan.

I will never forget my first week in the classroom with Dapper Dan. He was a skinny, small boy with a gorgeous smile seen far too infrequently. One day Dan decided he was not going to go to lunch with the other children. He proceeded to latch onto his desk with his head inside and didn't come out. Dan remained in his desk the entire morning. It was soon time for lunch but there was no one to help. What was I to do? The only option I had was to carry Dan, his chair and desk to the principal's office on the way to lunch.

I looked very much like a mother duck as I carried Dan and desk, followed by twenty-five first graders, down the hall, through the secretary's office and into Principal Kovatch's office. Mr. Kovatch was shocked, to say the least. He said very little; his eyes told the story. We left Dan. No more than five minutes later Dan walked into the cafeteria with Mr. Kovatch, wearing the biggest smile I had ever seen. He decided he was hungry and simply wanted to go to lunch with everyone else.

Dan continued to be a very difficult child, throughout the year requiring constant special attention. From that day on, I knew that whatever he did, if I could get Dan to smile that gorgeous smile, everything was right with the world.

Years later, Dan came to visit me at school. He stood before the class wearing his Navy uniform and his beautiful smile. I asked Dan to speak to the class.

He shared with the class that there were only two people he admired in his life: his grandmother and Mr. Schmitz. He shared too; that he was home to attend his grandmother's funeral and that he had come to school to tell me how very important I was in his life. Then and there, in front of the class, he thanked me.

It was the best thank-you I have ever received.

Ideas & suggestions
for parents

1. What do you see in the mirror?

Talk to your partner or a friend about how they see your relationship with your children. Ask them to describe what they observe and listen to what they have to say. Celebrate what you have accomplished and determine where you want to go:

- How is their observation different from yours?
- When you are ready to look seriously at your refection, what do you see?
- What do you like and what do you want to change?

2. Encouraging mentors

Grandparents, teachers, uncles, aunts, and friends are in a natural position to be mentors for your child. Second to trial and error, mentoring is the best way for a child to learn. Discuss with your child the following questions:

- Who do you see as a mentor in your life?
- Would you like to spend more time with them?
- What would you like to learn from your mentor?

3. Your vision for your children

Parents want something better for their children; each of us has a different vision of what that looks like. By looking in the mirror, we can learn a great deal about how we influence our children:

- What experiences shaped who you are?
- What values did your parents impart to you that you want to share with your children?
- What are your favorite childhood memories?
- Are your children extensions of yourself?

Ideas & suggestions
for grandparents

1. Write a story together

You enjoy reading with your grandchildren, so why not collaborate and write a short story together? Agree that each person will contribute the same amount of writing and that no one has the right to edit the other person's work:

- Mutually agree on the story title.
- Decide what you the story to be about.
- Determine a time to work on the story.
- Reflect on what you've learned about each other.

2. Volunteer

Children learn volunteering by example. Volunteering is a way of showing your appreciation for services provided to you and your family. Use the following questions to determine where you might like to volunteer:

- What community service do you value most?
- Do you or your child or grandchild share an interest where you could both volunteer?
- What skills are you not using today that you might like to share outside your normal day-to-day activities?
- Are there skills you would like to learn?
- What can you learn about other cultures by volunteering?

Crafts provide a wonderful opportunity for time together.

8

The four L's of effective Parent & Grandparent Relationships:

Loving,
Laughing,
Learning,
Listening

"Where there is love there is life."
— Mahatma Gandhi

Loving

The consensus among both parents and grandparents, when asked about the essential ingredients of effective relationships were loving, laughing, learning and listening. By practicing the 4 L's, parents and grandparents can build and maintain adult-child-grandchild-grandparent relationships.

Love in action

In order to love others you must first love yourself. I call this "self-love." Self-love is the process of learning to love yourself and believing you are worthy of being loved.

Love is a verb. When we embody self-love, we "take action" and share it with others. Grandparents and parents are in a unique position to "take action" and share themselves with their children and grandchildren.

Those around us nourish our love of self.

"Self-love is like a soft cushion of densely woven fabric around our core self, acting as a buffer against serious harm."

It provides us with an identity and clarifies for us who we are. Self-love is usually obtained and sustained through positive reinforcement from others and often from those we care about. We have a responsibility to share our love with others. In the act of sharing, we grow in self-love.

Those of us who have experienced love may have a sufficient amount of self-love, but many of us never received enough love and we spend a lifetime seeking it out.

"The 4 L's form the cornerstones of your relationship."

Grandparents and parents can build or destroy self-love. If a child is abused, laughed at or ignored, he or she will not feel self-love. Loving ourselves and appreciating who we are and what we are capable of is an ongoing lesson throughout our lives.

Self-love is learned from someone who cares. It doesn't just happen nor can we experience it on our own:

Mom and Dad were driving down the road attempting to talk to one another. They were having great difficulty hearing each other because their two children were arguing in the back seat. Finally, the frustrated mother turned around and yelled, "Love each other, damn it!" If only it was that simple!

How do we learn self-love?

When someone important in our lives tells or shows us they care about us, we feel special. We learn love of self through the love of another. This someone could be a parent, grandparent, brother, sister, teacher, spouse, neighbor, friend or a child.

> "Grandparents are better than parents. They always love me no matter what I do."
> — *Grandchild*

Recall how you felt in the following situations. Who did you share this experience with? Did that person reinforce your self-love?

- Getting your first bike
- Arm-wrestling with your dad and winning
- Scoring the most points in a game
- Singing in the choir
- Winning an award
- Getting your driver's license
- Graduating from college
- Bringing home your first big paycheck
- Surviving an illness

You demonstrate through actions your love. This demonstration of love promotes self-love:

- Travel out of state to witness the graduation of your grandchild.
- Attend your son's hockey game when you're exhausted.
- Be there for a friend after the loss of his parent
- Chaperone a high school dance for your son, the night before a 6:00 AM departure for a business trip.
- Drive three hundred miles to attend your granddaughter's dance recital.
- Help your child with the down payment on his first car.

When we practice giving and receiving self-love, we will begin to understand ourselves and open our hearts to our children and grandchildren's love. We can discover what others love about us when we are open to looking within. Unconditional love can make a difference:

- Whether you succeed or fail, I love you.
- I believe in you and know you will learn from whatever happens.
- Thank you.
- I love you despite your behavior.
- You may not have won but you did your best and that is what matters.

Self-love is one of the most important lessons parents or grandparents can teach. Each time we are there to support our children, for who they are, everyone benefits.

Love has different eyes

Sam, whose face was peppered with freckles, and his Grandma were spending the day at the zoo. Long lines of children were waiting to have their faces painted.

A little girl next to Sam announced, "You've got so many freckles, there's no place to paint!"

Embarrassed, Sam dropped his head. His grandmother knelt down next to him. "I love your freckles, they make you special. When I was a little girl, I always wanted freckles. Freckles are beautiful."

Sam looked up, "Really?" he said hesitantly.

"Oh, yes, just name one thing prettier than freckles?" Sam thought for a moment and looked directly at his grandmother's face and whispered softly "Wrinkles."

Teach your children to love themselves

An outcome of the women's rights movement is the increased involvement of both parents in the daily lives of their children. Freeing the mother from being the sole caregiver has brought about a major change in the way children have been raised. Many parents believe they are equal partners in the process of teaching self-love to their children. Children need the experience of being taught self-love by both the male and female gender.

> "Love has nothing to do with what you receive; it's what you give."
> — *Anonymous*

A child learns self-love from both parents. Many mothers now make significant financial contributions to their families and fathers are being counted on more than in the past to raise the children. This is true not only in America, but other parts of the world. In Sweden, both fathers and mothers take paternity/maternity leave, when their children are born. The positive effect of both parents' involvement will be an increase in the concept, understanding and teaching of self-love. Our quality of life and the future of our society are dependent upon on how well we teach our children love of self.

Appropriate touch

Self-love can be reinforced by appropriate touch. Unfortunately, touch, in our society has become a sensitive topic. We are horrified at the numerous cases of abuse through inappropriate touch. Rather than place a moratorium on touching, it is more important than ever that children are taught appropriate touch. Instead of abandoning all forms of touch, we need to learn when hugs and other forms of affection are appropriate. Hugs are an outward sign that someone cares, appreciates and supports who we are. We should teach our children appropriate expressions of affection through touch.

> "As we are liberated from our own fear, our presence automatically liberates others."
> — *Nelson Mandela*

As a former first grade teacher, I experienced first-hand how the positive use of touch could be a valuable reward and a meaningful form of self-love for a child. Teachers would often greet the children in the morning and say good-bye at the end of the day with a hug. Each time a hug was given, no matter what had happened in class, the child would smile. These hugs are so often needed to counter balance the tough circumstances that children face. Our society and especially our children are starved for appropriate touch.

In the late 1980s, as a result of the inappropriateness of a few, our society discouraged all forms of touch. Mandates prohibiting touch were given to institutions working with children.

Unfortunately, hugging and other forms of touch became associated with abuse and molestation. We now have a generation of children who have grown up with limited experience in the appropriate use of touch.

It is more important than ever to teach the value of appropriate touching or hugging and to model hugging as a valuable form of self-love.

Adults need hugs as well. When hugs are appropriately given, you can feel the comfort deep within. Some adult males find giving hugs to other men difficult. Men need encouragement and support in giving and receiving hugs. Recently, while playing in a father-son golf tournament, I visited with an old friend and greeted him with a hug. I felt great but I could tell my friend was uncomfortable.

Fear, the enemy of self-love

Fear stops us from reaching our full potential. If we haven't been taught how to make good choices, we become vulnerable. Others will put us down, question our abilities, our character or our motives. When we are fearful, we look to others for answers.

Children need adults to empower them to make choices. If our fears or need to control do not tolerate choice, in the end, we provide a serious disservice to the child.

"Support from within the family embraces our self-love and acts as the armor for whatever obstacles they may encounter."

Love is sometimes saying nothing at all

Have you given unsolicited advice to your child or grandchild? Was that advice appreciated or necessary?

"Laughing signifies pleasure, comfort, and enjoyment; it's contagious."

No one person has the right to control another. Some parents and grandparents prevent children from making decisions that they perceive as detrimental to their well being. When we learn to say nothing at all, we provide a child with the opportunity to own the rewards and the consequences of their decision. Allowing others to make choices is the ultimate form of respect. Giving choices encourages the child to accept responsibility for his actions and the experience to make better decisions in the future.

"Let go and trust; it sets the stage for growth."

It's a true act of love when parents or grandparents silently allow an adult child or grandchild to make a choice that is contrary to the way the parent and grandparent would do it. The next time you want to give unsolicited advice to your child or grandchild ask yourself:

- Do you believe your loved one is intelligent?
- Have they demonstrated the ability to make other decisions?
- Is your advice self-serving? Do you want to feel important?
- Will you lose or gain the confidence of your child or grandchild?
- Are you providing your child the opportunity to grow?

When we respect each other's choices, we are truly wise.

Infant wisdom

Grandpa and granddaughter, Sara, had a weekly ritual. Every Saturday morning they would walk to the local restaurant for breakfast. They had their favorite booth next to the front door. Invariably, some of Grandpa's friends would pass by and tell Sara what a pretty girl she was, and how lucky Grandpa was to have such a nice granddaughter! This made Sara very happy.

Upon returning home one Saturday, Grandma asked, "Why do you like going to breakfast with Grandpa?"

Sara replied, "When I am with my Grandpa—everybody loves me!" *Grandpa Group*

Laughing

The insight of a very wise ninety-year-old grandmother:

"The first place to start building any relationship is on the other person's level. When children are young, you need to be young too. I like to imagine the world through their eyes and there, quickly find something to laugh about."

Have you ever walked past a room full of people laughing? Don't you just want to get in there and be a part of it? Children bring laughter and enjoyment to our lives. They seem to be able to bring a sense of youthfulness to grandparents. There is no better sound than a child's laughter. If you can make a child laugh, you have brought music into the world.

It's a well-known fact that ten minutes of belly laughing will reduce stress and help you sleep. Children are the best source of belly laughs. Grandchildren are all about fun and are drawn to people who are fun.

I've always admired people who can tell jokes well. Some people are adept at bringing jokes into ordinary conversations; it is a wonderful gift. If this is your gift, use it with your grandchildren. The more simple the joke, such as a knock-knock joke, the sillier it becomes and the more laughter it generates.

> "Laughter is two hearts tickling one another." — *Grandparent group*

Sending jokes in the mail is a quick way to brighten someone's day. Today it is convenient to share jokes in cards and e-mails. Children of all ages love jokes and riddles and they gain self-esteem when they can tell a good joke. Sometimes it's difficult for an adult to wait for a child to complete the joke, but being patient contributes greatly to a child's feeling of accomplishment. They deserve your time and appreciation and laughing is a wonderful way to give them your attention.

Laughing at a joke is a way to show respect. We tend to laugh with people when we respect them.

"When I was four-years-old, I told a joke to my Grandfather and he laughed and laughed.

Later that day, Grandpa Ed and I walked across the street to visit his neighbor and my grandfather asked me to repeat the joke. I told it better than ever.

Many years later, I don't remember the joke but I will never forget how I felt. I felt so important . . . so valued . . . so loved.

*I love to tell jokes and make people laugh. I attribute this to
my grandfather."*

What better reason is there to laugh than to laugh with our
grandchildren? Laughing together just feels good and when
you have someone to share it with, the good feelings multiply.
My grandchildren help me laugh and help me to know who I
am. Smiles are simple ways to show unconditional acceptance.
The most memorable days of our lives are the ones we spent
laughing.

"What a simple powerful gift a smile can be!"

Get grandkids to laugh

We don't need to tell the stories; in fact, it's better when your
grandchildren tell the stories. Put your grandchildren on
stage and take a seat in the audience.

*"When Max is really happy he says, 'Come on, let's dance!'
When he is finished, I say, 'Let's do it all over again and we
laugh some more'"*

When my grandchildren tell me stories, I show I'm listening
by saying encouraging words, "Wow!" . . . "No joke!" . . . "Can
you say that with your eyes closed?" or, "Oh my goodness, tell
that story again!" "Can you tell that story again while squeez-
ing your nose?" "You are so funny!"

Use "encouraging words" frequently. The moment is propelled
forward and everyone feels even better about who they are.

We learn from our grandparents. Grandma Judy has always
been complimented on her contagious laugh.

*"Saturday was my favorite day of the week, the time I went to
my Grandma's and Grandpa's house. As soon as I would get in*

*the door, my grandfather would grab me, tickle me and make
me laugh. Years later, when he was about to leave this earth,
I asked Grandpa why he did that. His answer was, 'I was just
being selfish. Whenever I would hear you laugh, it made me
laugh, too.'*

*Today, I'm the one giggling with my grandchildren and I
constantly receive compliments on my laugh. I've realized, it's
not my laugh at all, but my Grandpa's."*

"Grandma, Jimmy isn't real"

*Grandma loved to make Cabbage Patch dolls for her grand-
daughters for Christmas. After Christmas, Grandma had a
doll left over that she placed under the Christmas tree next to
a toy dog.*

*Grandson Shawn, who was five years old, came over for a
visit. When he saw the doll he asked, "What's the name of your
doll?"*

*Grandma answered, "Oh, that's Jimmy, he keeps me com-
pany when you're not here".*

Shaun, still curious asked, "Well, whose dog is that?"

*Grandma again answered, "Oh that dog belongs to the doll
Jimmy, he needs a friend too."*

*Shawn was a little confused by this time and had a strange
look on his face.*

*Finally he said, "Well, can I play with them?" Grandma
answered, "Oh sure you can."*

*When it was time to go home. Shawn gave Grandma a kiss
on the cheek and said, "Grandma, I have to tell you something, you know that doll Jimmy, he isn't real and you know
something else, neither is his dog!"*

Life can get too serious. When one grandmother wants to "get lighthearted" with her grandchildren she tells "Grandma-was-a-little-girl" stories. "I often get hysterical over the ridiculous things I did. They love to hear me tell stories about their parents, brothers and sisters. The more the old stories are told, the more they become embellished. The more we exaggerate the story, the more they love it." It is good for everyone when we laugh about our childhood antics.

Another grandmother described laughing with her grandchildren:

"I thoroughly enjoy hearing my granddaughter laugh. It brings me sheer delight even when it's not funny."

Infant wisdom

Grandpa Norm was talking to his granddaughter and sharing some of the fun things he did as a boy; "We had a tire swing in our back yard and we could go really high! We grew our own raspberries and made jam. I took my calf to the fair and won a blue ribbon!"

Finally, granddaughter Sarah interrupted him and said, "I sure wish I would have known you when you were a boy!"

Embarrassing moments

A very wise grandfather shared the following: "Whenever things get boring, I tell stories from the past and the more embarrassing the story is, the more my grandchildren laugh and the better I feel."

Isn't that the truth? The more embarrassing our story is, the more the children feel connected to us. Our stories remind grandchildren of themselves and teach them that everyone makes mistakes, gets embarrassed, and yet survives. Laughing at ourselves is a valuable skill to acquire early in life. Any time we learn something new; we must be willing to suffer uncertainty and embarrassment. When we can laugh at ourselves, we become more comfortable with who we are.

> "Laughing with children is like pillow fights from the heavens — rolling in the soft feathery plumes as they fall to the ground."
>
> — *Grandparent group*

Stories that start with, "The time I came home late from a date" or "The time I didn't listen to my parents" or "When I ripped my Sunday pants" are wonderful ways to initiate laughter. When we tell our "human, embarrassing" stories, our grandchildren feel more comfortable sharing their stories.

Grandma Sue endured her embarrassing school days and grew up to raise seven incredible children. Her twenty-three grandchildren eighteen great grandchildren laugh and enjoy her stories today.

School Days

"I was born on a farm in Dundas, Minnesota, the oldest of eight children. I spoke German until I went to school. I remember going to school the first day and being teased for not knowing any English. "One day, when I was at school, my ma and pa drove by with the horses and I yelled in German, "There go my Mom and Dad!" I was the laughingstock of the playground. I remember three older boys who laughed at me. I am eighty-seven years old and I can remember their names to this day. I learned to speak English fast!

One day, while I was sitting in the outhouse, I noticed a beam of light shining on me through the wall. The boys had figured out a way to remove one of the knots in the wall and were peeking in at me through the knothole. I fixed them; I went and told the teacher and the boys had to split wood for the rest of the week!

In those days, we all wore underwear called bloomers; or goldybukz. My mother made our bloomers out of yellow flour sacks. They consisted of a piece of elastic around the waist and two other pieces of elastic just above the knees. The boys used to love to tease us when we fell. They would shout at us, 'I can see your goldybukz, I can see your goldybukz!' I was so embarrassed.

I remember other fun things too: learning how to gather maple syrup in the spring in Gillens' woods, chasing striped gophers, hauling wood in for the fire and playing hide and go seek.

"Two years behind me in school was a cute little boy named Eddie. I liked him from the start; later he became my husband. We recently celebrated our sixty-third wedding anniversary and I still like that little boy!"

Not everyone can share stories that expose their "humanness." In the movie, "Nobody's Fool," Paul Newman plays the part of a grandfather in his late 50s who had ignored his family all his life but discovers he cares a great deal for his grandson. His son can't believe the change in his father and asks, "If you were never a father to me, why do you want to be a grandfather to my son?" Paul's reply was, "Cause you've got to start someplace."

Parents can spend so much of their parenting years providing for the ever-growing list of basics that they seldom find time for laughing and good old-fashioned fun. They say that grandparenting an opportunity for us to start over and do it right. As Paul Newman said, "You have to start someplace."

Learning and relearning

Our children and grandchildren can keep us young and provide opportunities for our personal growth. When we are childlike, our authentic self is released and we forget our fears. The challenge of learning, relearning and unearthing our creativity can be uncomfortable. Act young and you'll feel young. Act old and you'll feel old.

Facing our fears will prevent fear from taking control.

An Indian chief had a young brave ask him for his advice. The young man was about to complete his final rite of passage. He was to be alone in the wilderness for one passing of the moon. Before he set out, he said to the chief, "I am afraid. I have two dogs within me; one says I will be able to accomplish my task and another says I won't. Which one will win? The chief answered, "The one who feeds your thoughts."

Infant wisdom

He's learning the sounds that animals make.

"Charlie, What does a cow say?"

"Moo."

"Charlie, What does a horse say?"

"Neigh, Neigh."

To satisfy our curiosity, we asked, "Charlie, what does your mommy say?"

Charlie hesitated for a second, then shouted, "Mommy says, 'No, No, No!'"

Like the young brave, if we focus on fear, it will control our destiny. We will never realize our dreams and fear will control us. Learning something new or relearning something we've forgotten inspires us to new heights. No one is destined to remain stagnant. We can choose to change, if we face our fear.

We will grow if we let go of thoughts and ideas that no longer work effectively. I like the analogy of a computer hard drive. When the hard-drive becomes full, the computer slows down and will not function at full capacity. If we don't throw out the worthless data and make room for new information, our thoughts and behaviors become stuck. Unfortunately, people can't go out and buy memory; instead we must learn to discard what no longer works for us. In the process, we discover new information that energizes and inspires us. In letting go, we gain freedom to move forward.

We've all witnessed the high-school athlete who stopped growing at the age of eighteen and believed his best years were behind him when his high

> "Learning is remembering what you already know."
> — *Plato*

school football career ended. We've witnessed the employee who begins his career and progresses rapidly for the first three years, then stops and is unhappy with his job for years. Sadly, we've observed burned out teachers and tenured professors, bored to death; too comfortable to risk change.

Children will not tolerate boredom and can inspire our growth. Parents and grandparents have an opportunity to grow with their children's energy and benefit from their shared experiences.

"'Bringing generations together' is mutually beneficial."

Our lives are like chapters in a book. Sometimes we get so involved, we think this chapter will last forever. Then an event occurs and a new chapter unfolds before us. In order for us to participate fully in the next chapter, we must be flexible and open to what this new chapter has to offer.

We experience opportunities and challenge with each chapter in our lives; getting married, having a child, losing a job, becoming a grandparent or experiencing the death of a parent. Our choice is to accept or fight the inevitable changes in our lives.

Infant wisdom

It was a cold winter morning, when Bella, age 3, woke up after spending one of her first nights at Grandpa's and Grandma's house. The windows were frosted and the snow was swirling across the yard ad she looked out the window.

After breakfast, Grandpa was getting ready for work. Grandma had made a fresh pot of coffee and poured it into Grandpa's Thermos bottle. As Grandpa was about to leave, Bella said, "Grandpa, don't forget your furnace, it's thirteen deblow."

Learn to begin again

Boomer grandparents have experienced more change than any of their ancestors. What will you do in the next chapter of your life?

- Continue in your present career
- Return to school
- Spend more time with family and friends

- Retire early and move to another state or country
- Stop working
- Pursue a new avocation
- Travel or live part-time in a second home
- Work part-time

Any one of the above decisions will prompt change and provide opportunities to begin again. For boomers, there are few mentors for the questions we suddenly are facing. Fortunately, one of the characteristics of boomers is that they have always done things their way, contrary to previous generations. There is no reason to think that as they become grandparents, this will change.

An unexpected circumstance that many boomers are facing today is the need to continue to work. A number of young grandparents, out of necessity, have delayed retirement or returned to work after watching slumping stock prices take a bite out of their retirement account. According to the recent Labor Department statistics, September 2002, "Forty percent of men 55 and older are still working and twenty-eight percent of women 55 and older remain in the workforce." This figure is a record high. It represents the highest percent of working men over 55, since January of 1984.

Other factors force men and women to continue to work: changes in government and company retirement plans; longer life expectancies, the need to shoulder additional retirement costs and higher medical bills. Despite men and women working longer, the number of years spent in retirement is likely to grow.

Grandparents are the support

A challenge for many grandparents is learning how to play a supporting role, not the lead character. A support person is a team player; a team player looks good when everyone else looks good. He's not the person in front of the TV camera, but rather the cameraman.

A supporting role can be a difficult adjustment for grandparents who have controlled their families. No one can assume that adult children and grandchildren should do what you think.

How we accept the supporting role will determine whether grandparenting will be a grand experience or a grand canyon.

Learn to be a witness

What would a celebration be without witnesses? One of the most important participants in a celebration is the witness. By their presence, witnesses acknowledge that there is something to celebrate. Their attendance adds to the significance of the event.

Parents and grandparents can be expert witnesses. A baby's first steps, the tooth under the pillow, the child's first bike ride, birthdays and the blue ribbon at the science fair are some of the

Infant wisdom

Six-year-old Isaac was sitting on a tree stump by the campfire eating his hot dog and chattering.

"This is the goodest camp I've ever been to . . .

"This is the goodest hot dog I've ever eaten."

As Camp Director, I was listening and laughing.

I asked, "Can I quote you on that?"

Isaac quickly responded, "No, I'm going to eat it!"

first opportunities we have to bear witness. Witnesses share in our successes and enhance their importance. Celebrations form the stepping-stones for events in our lives. How important would a wedding or graduation be with no one present to bear witness?

> "Real joy starts when I let go of my agenda and get on my grandchild's agenda."
> — *Grandparent Group*

We can celebrate the little things: finishing a class, learning to play a piece on the piano, watching the sun come up in the morning or the wind blowing through the trees.

Grandparent truths

- Having a child in your arms brings peace to your heart.
- A walk around the block with a grandchild is insurance for a good night's sleep.
- The more children ignore you, the more they want your attention.
- You are suddenly a whole lot smarter around your grandchildren than you were around your children.
- It's healthy to be goofy with your grandchild.
- Smiling is the best way to communicate your love.
- A grandchild's hand hooks your heart as well as your hand.
- The gifts we don't receive may be the best presents of all.
- Listening to a child breathe is one of the most comforting sounds you will ever hear.

Listening

When you respect your children and grandchildren, they will respect you. Active listening is proof that you care and value them. Often, if our conclusions are incorrect, it is because we didn't listen carefully or we jumped in with solutions, opinions and judgments. When something seems confusing, we need to ask for clarification. Responding to what you thought you heard can lead to further miscommunication. It's better to delay a response than give an immediate answer you will later regret.

The relationship, or lack of relationship, with our children and grandchildren affects our understanding of who they are. I compare it to talking to my great aunt who couldn't hear very well. It became so difficult for her to hear anyone that few people bothered to try to talk to her.

Listen to your adult child

Treat your adult children as adults. We communicate not only through our voice but our facial expressions and body language. When grandparents use a demeaning tone with their adult child in their communication it is insurance for poor communication. Adult children deserve to be treated as adults with equal status. Not validating what a child has to say may give you the false sense of control but, in most cases, the child will simply stop trying to communicate.

Mutual respect requires a high degree of listening skills. Parents have to learn to listen to their children as adults. Adult children have to re-learn how to listen to their parents and not allow themselves to be thrown back into their childhood when communicating with their parents.

Men are often criticized for not listening. In the popular book, Men are From Mars and Women Are From Venus, John Gray repeatedly talks about how men try to provide solutions.

They think they are listening when they attempt to provide solutions. Men often make the mistake of attempting to fix what their children and grandchildren share with them. This is not what their children and grandchildren are looking for. They want someone to respect them, care enough to listen

> "A good listener tries to understand what another person is saying. In the end he may disagree, but before he does, he knows what he is disagreeing with."
> — *Kenneth A. Wells,* author of
> *New God New Nation*

and be a sounding board. We show respect when we believe that someone is capable of finding his or her own solutions.

A self-test for effective listening

- Do you or your child feel guarded in conversation?
- Do you ask your children for their opinions?
- Is your tone different when you talk to a child?
- Do you walk away from difficult conversations?
- Do you ask your child for help in understanding?
- Does your child seek your help and guidance?
- Do you interrupt your child?
- Do you ask questions for clarification?
- Do you look at your child when they speak?
- Do you presume to know what your child has to say and not actually listen to what they want to share?
- Do you ask questions that will support them in finding their own answers?
- Do you attempt to tell them what to do?

Turn off your control button

Listening doesn't involve coercion. We don't all see the world in the same way: isn't that wonderful? Allow your children and grandchildren to talk with little or no feedback. When we listen with our full attention, we lay ourselves open to new and valuable thoughts.

By showing respect and listening carefully, we demonstrate that our "control" button is turned "off." Attentive listening is proof to the child that we love and respect them. When we feel what your child has to say, in our heart, we have actively listened.

> "I honor my children's choices as to how they want to raise their children, and follow their lead."
> — *Grandparent Group*

Practicing good listening is the best way for a grandparent to gain a grandchild's trust. You will know you are a good listener when your grandchild seeks you out to talk with them.

We show we care when we:

- Give children undivided attention.
- Don't interrupt.
- Ask questions that help clarify.
- Avoid generalizations and opinions.
- Avoid judgments.
- Avoid comparisons with other children, grandchildren, nieces and nephews.
- Don't take everything (including ourselves) too seriously.
- Are careful when teasing.
- Don't take your family for granted.
- Use a sense of humor.

An effective grandparent:

- Mentors and guides.
- Is a friend and listener.
- Understands priorities and what is or is not worth making an issue.
- Knows that even though an incident may appear insignificant, if it's important to the child, it's important.
- Laughs and loves unconditionally.
- Follows the family rules.
- Validates and encourages while tossing in a bit of humor.

Ideas & suggestions
for parents

1. Assess your parenting skills

To find out how successful you are as a parent, ask your child the following questions and be prepared to listen. Keep an open mind and look at the responses as opportunities for you to grow. Resist being defensive and set goals to be a more effective parent:

· Do you think I understood how you feel?
· What do I do, that you would like me to do more often?
· When was the last time I told you how proud I am of you?
· What would you like us to do more of together?
· When have I disappointed you?

2. Parents are builders

Effective parents provide encouragement and "build" their children with self-love and choices. Look at the ways you show your children encouragement and support. What words do you use? Are your children feeling supported?

If not, support them with self-love statements:

• I am so proud of you!
• I knew you could do it! Let me see you do it again
• Remember how good you felt when . . .
• I could never do that when I was your age

3. Have fun with your children

Too often as parents we are required to be disciplinarians. Make an effort to have fun with your children. Let them see your lighter side. Being a parent can also mean having fun. Try this:

- As you are driving in the car or sitting at the dinner table, share a funny thing that happened to you.
- Describe for your children how you felt when you first realized you were in love with their mother or father. Encourage their questions.
- Describe times when you were mischievous and got caught.
- Tell your children about your mistakes.
- Tell them about someone who hurt your feelings and how you felt .
- Encourage your children to tell their own stories.

4. How can grandparents help parents?

Invite your parents to be involved. You are in charge of this "great resource" grandparents. Who has a more vested interest in the well being of your child?

Frustrated, exhausted parents need a sounding board and parents can provide this. They have experience.

If you have multiple sets of grandparents who want to be involved, additional planning may be necessary. Parents, talk to grandparents about their involvement and be clear about what they can expect.

Ideas & suggestions
for grandparents

1. Reconciliation with adult children

Despite our best intentions, we make mistakes. Things happen; devastating things we never intended. It's never too late for reconciliation. If you are seeking a relationship with your grandchild, begin with the parents. Reconciliation takes time and work. You can lay the seeds for reconciliation by acknowledging your part. Denial will only lead to additional conflict and separation. Forgive and ask for forgiveness.

2. Giving and receiving

Material gifts are not what grandchildren need or remember. What is remembered is your gift of time. The best gifts are the activities you engage in with your grandchildren instead of for them. Do things *with* them, not *for* them.

Continual correspondence and activities at a very early age, even from a distance, is necessary to become a part of your grandchildren's lives.

Send cards, letters, emails and pictures to maintain your relationships while apart.

Ask questions in your letters that require a response. Demonstrate that you know or have some knowledge of what interests them. If you don't know, find out.

3. Listen more

Make a goal to learn something new about each member of your family. To have a rewarding exchange, use open-ended questions like:

"Tell me about . . . "

"How does it make you feel when . . . "

"Can you tell me more about . . . "

To remember what was shared, write it down and keep it in their file. Recap the information and share it with other members of the family.

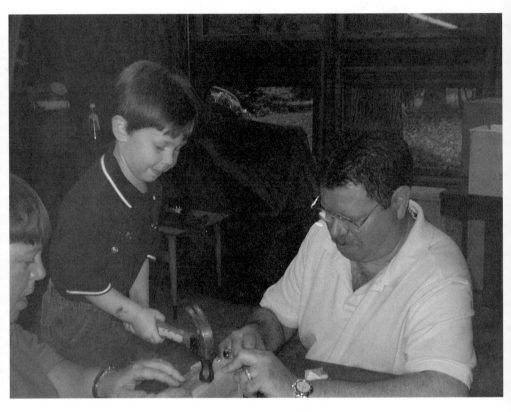

When Grandparents Support

9

Making family work

Expect the unexpected

Each year we assess the condition of our vehicle, have a physical examination and do our taxes. Yet how often do we plan for our most important asset, our family? For many of us, the answer is that we don't plan at all. Family life just happens. When crises or major change occurs, we are often ill prepared to handle them.

When we do financial planning, we start by asking questions and conducting some basic research. We seek professional help, an accountant or financial advisor. Finally, we take the necessary steps to put a plan in place. I suggest you take a similar approach with your family plan.

Begin by talking with your family:

- How important is family to you?
- What happens if there is an unexpected death or serious illness in the family?

- Are you willing to commit time and energy to your family?
- What are you doing to maintain your relationships with your family?
- How are you preparing for the time when your children leave home, go to college, move across the country, get married or experience a crisis?
- What is your relationship with your extended family?
- What will be your role if a parent becomes ill or dies?
- How do you handle individual differences within the family?

The answers to these questions will identify your priorities and get you started on creating a family plan.

Just like your financial plan, it will need to be modified as circumstances change. If you anticipate conflict, consider calling in professionals now. Professionals can include: a minister or priest, a personal coach, family planner or counselor.

Longevity and grandparenting

Boomer grandparents have an opportunity to do something many of our grandparents never lived long enough to experience: share time, beliefs and values with your children's children and very likely their children. In the last century, medical science has made significant advances that contribute to longer life expectancy. The result is that many of us will have the opportunity to lead healthy and productive lives well into our 80s and 90s.

The next generations will be the first in which a majority of children will know and have a relationship with their great-grandparents. Great-grandparents will be pioneers in their relationships to family and society, a position with few role models.

A large number of grandparents will live to see their grandchildren as adults. Your children will have the opportunity to seek the expertise of their parents as they approach their own retirement. As the role of grandparents and great-grandparents extends into multiple generations, we will have the opportunity to create new, multigenerational relationships.

In addition to helping their immediate families, grandparents will continue to be active in their communities. Once communities realize the vital resource they have in their aging, educated population, more opportunities will emerge for grandparents and great-grandparents to impact their communities.

A grandson's reflection on Grandpa

If you have ever been to my parents' home, you'll remember a prominent display of family pictures covering the wall of the staircase. In this collection of pictures, you will find babies, graduations, weddings and family portraits.

Last Sunday, not long after hearing the news of Grandpa's death, something moved me to sit at the foot of these stairs. Not more than two feet from me was Grandpa's engagement photo, a great picture of a young handsome man.

As I stared at his picture, more than sixty years old, something inside me told me he wasn't just smiling for the photograph; he was smiling directly at me. At that moment, the grief I was experiencing disappeared. He was telling me that everything was all right and he was in a better place.

We all love you Grandpa. You are in our hearts and you will always be with us.

Your loving grandson,
S.

"Going it alone" doesn't work well for anyone

Our culture places too much pressure on parents to raise their children. With one-third of our grandparents being "Parents Forever" and one-third of our grandparents being "Help When Asked," we have two-thirds of the grandparent population willing to help. So, why aren't more parents asking for assistance?

A cooperative study conducted by the YMCA and the Search Institute found fifty-three percent of young parents do not seek support from their families. This survey also found that thirty-one percent turn to their families, eleven percent turn to friends and four percent use community resources.

Jim believed he was totally responsible for his children. This belief worked well until one day his son fell off the swing at the playground. Jim and his wife were at work. If it hadn't been for a neighborhood father providing first aid and calling the local hospital, there is no telling what might have happened to Jim's son. Jim's awareness was changed. He now knows there is a community available and willing to support him and his family.

As children, we were indoctrinated with the importance of being responsible for ourselves. We became adults only when we could take care of ourselves. It appears this independence is keeping us from seeking help even when it is desperately needed. Everyone stands to benefit when we seek the help of family, friends and community. When parents choose to "go it alone," they shun the opportunity to "Bring Generations Together" and minimize the possibility of some very important relationships.

At the age of 84, Julio volunteers as a reading coach at a neighborhood elementary school three hours, one day a week. When asked why he did it, he responded, "When I went to this school, I had a hard time learning to read and I don't want children to go through life the way I did. I feel valued here and I think the kids like having me around."

Grandparents can be a critical component in the volunteer network. Are we overlooking this valuable resource?

Conflict in families

Family conflicts have been documented ever since stories were first written. The Bible often told these stories. So what can we do to resolve conflict in the family?

In a perfect world, when young families need help, grandparents are there to provide it. Grandparent involvement is beneficial for everyone. Children benefit from multiple mentors and loving adult companionship. Parents enjoy an adult relationship with their parents. Grandparents can provide wisdom, support and a much-needed break for parents. Grandparents are stimulated by the youthful energy of their grandchildren. Children provide love, laughter, and often a whole "other world" of intellectual awareness for grandparents.

Often parents fail to seek help and support from their family because they fear judgment or conflict. They choose to raise their children themselves rather than work through family misunderstandings and disagreements. As a result of this isolation, families grow further apart.

It is no surprise our young families are feeling overwhelmed. Divorce, addiction, interracial marriage, adoption, blended families, illness and chemical dependency all fuel conflict in families. Combine this with parents working longer hours, an increasing number of single parents and grandparents living far from their children and grandchildren.

Sarah was a single grandmother with two adult married sons. She enjoyed spending time with her sons and their families, when suddenly her world changed. One son's divorce and subsequent remarriage presented her with a new daughter-in-law and two young step-grandchildren. Time with her beloved grandchildren became more and more difficult to arrange. She felt awkward around her former daughter-in-law and found it difficult to communicate with her new daughter-in-law and step-grandchildren. Her son became frustrated and angry at his mother's treatment of his wife and children. Sarah wanted things the way they were. Relaxation and enjoyment had given way to resentment and guilt. Sarah's once congenial family disappeared.

Stories like Sarah's are played out in homes across the country on a daily basis. Often the issues involve favoritism, resentment, misunderstanding, prejudice and guilt. When problems go unresolved, families are pulled apart.

Blended families and conflict

Blended families are defined as a family made up of a minimum of two children in which one member comes from a previous relationship. In the United States, blended families now exceed the number of biological families as the norm. With the growth of blended families comes the potential for increased conflict. Some problems may be deep seated and require intervention by a trained professional.

Grandparents find themselves thrust into unfamiliar roles with little experience. Growing older often translates into anyone or anything that is "different." As we age, we fail to see uniqueness as something that is less than positive. An acceptance of "different" and unfamiliar is needed.

Parents and grandparent can reduce conflict by agreeing to communicate. Problem-solving and conflict-resolution skills, combined with a willingness to attempt proposed solutions are key to resolving difficulties.

The issues between parents and their adult children can be compounded when we attempt to offer advice during a time of crisis. Unfortunately, even though we are well aware of this fact, we forget in the heat of the moment. We must strive to be patient, choose an appropriate time, speak directly and honestly and then listen.

Never attempt to deal with conflict when you are tired or overwhelmed. Everyone gets tired: grandparents, parents and grandchildren. Choose a time when everyone is well rested. If the time isn't right, back away and say nothing at all.

When conflict occurs:

1. Remember to respect your children's decisions.
2. Provide support; do not force your methods or beliefs on your adult children.
3. Respect the ability and capacity of your children to be parents.
4. Complement parents on the job they are doing.
5. Remember, parents make the rules.

When you accept our family's differences we also recognize our strengths. Resolving conflict helps our children, grandchildren and our communities.

The effect of divorce on children

Grandparents can be a sanctuary for their grandchildren during divorce. They can provide a "home away from home" where grandchildren can talk, temporarily forget their pain and enjoy the nurturing of their grandparents. It is a critical time for grandparents to express their love and concern. Everyone needs extra gentle attention at this difficult time.

During divorce, parents are so focused on their own feelings of loss, anger and change that they do not have the capacity to provide the love and attention their children deserve. They understand their situation but don't have the emotional stability to provide for their children.

Parents must be able to deal with their own anger before attempting to help their children.

"I love my children, but I just want them to go away. I have no patience and often yell at them for no reason. When I yell, it makes me feel even worse. My problems are bad enough and I don't want to pass them on, but I am."

Divorce affects children differently depending upon the age, gender and the parents' behavior. Younger children tend to adjust to divorce easier and teenagers have the most difficulty. Children don't care if love is right or wrong, they want love. During, and long after divorce, the children will experience feelings of sadness. They want things to be the way they were but are powerless to make it happen. Anger and changes in behavior can occur in children without the child's parent's knowledge.

Grandparents need to be alert to children's changing moods. Children experience grief similar to the grief caused by death. They worry that they are the reason for their parents' problems and that their parents don't love them anymore. Everyone is on edge, it's important to stay as calm as possible, not overreact and be sensitive to the needs of the children.

A special challenge for grandparents is to avoid making

negative comments about their son or daughter's former spouse. Parents and grandparents both need to keep in mind that "little ears" may be listening when adults are talking about the divorce, either in person or on the phone. Children can misinterpret a statement like, "I just want to run away and be alone." There is no telling the effect such a statement might have on the child. Never overlook the intuitive and perceptive capacity of a child.

Grandparent's role in divorce

There is no single answer for dealing with your adult children and grandchildren's pain during the time of divorce. Each family must discover its own path, but concern, empathy and love displayed in a variety of ways by both the parents and grandparents are important.

If grandparents can remain neutral in their involvement, they will be in a better position to assist their children and grandchildren.

During this critical time, a grandparent needs to be a model of unconditional love for the parents and the grandchildren. Remember that even though your child is in pain and you would like to help them, what is needed

> "I love my Grandma! When I go to her house she drops everything she's doing and I become her total focus."
> *Grandma Group*

most is your love and unconditional support.

Some grandparents spend extra time with the children or even take the children on vacation. Other grandparents may choose to help by making frequent short visits and bringing simple gifts to express their love and temporarily distract from the pain. It's important for the parents and grandchildren to know that they are part of a bigger family, that they have not been abandoned and that they are still loved. It's a good time to seek the help of the extended family: uncles, aunts and neighbors.

An eight-year-old girl shared the following experience after her parents' divorce:

"It was during the time of my parents' divorce that I learned to really love my grandparents. I remember my grandfather asking about my feelings and then really listening to me. I knew and felt his love."

Step-grandparenting

An often-overlooked member of the blended family is the step-grandparent. As more people begin and end marriages, we can expect to have more step-grandchildren and step-grandparents.

According to Serena Plunkett from the University of Missouri-Columbia, "Approximately 33% of all persons sixty-five and older are step-grandparents," and this number is growing. Whether we like it or not, step-grandparenting is with us to stay. We need to encourage these adopted grandparents' involvement in the family.

Like grandparenting, we won't be effective step-grandparents until we have some experience. It's important to become involved as soon as possible though that may be challenging. Some step-grandchildren are young adults when they become part of a new family and may not be open to step-grandparents.

Though step-grandparenting may make life a little more complex and confusing, the effort to develop a relationship with your "new family" can be beneficial for everyone.

Jim and Kathy married when they were fifty-five years old. Both had children and grandchildren and wanted to be involved grandparents to all their grandchildren, treating their step-grandchildren and their grandchildren alike. As a couple, they had six grandchildren. Because the grandchildren had a relationship with one of the grandparents, the grandchildren were able to accept this new grandparent quite easily.

Kathy and Jim believed that it was one another's responsibility to assist each other in getting to know their grandchildren. They started by going to the grandchildren's homes and eventually made the transition of having all the grandchildren to their home. They discovered the grandchildren enjoyed spending time with their larger blended family.

A challenge for step-grandparents is not the number of additional grandchildren, but accommodating all the grandparents. This is especially true over the holidays. It's vitally important that competition does not occur between grandparents. Be flexible and accommodating in your plans. It may not be ideal, but it is the time spent together that is most important. Criticisms of the "other" grandparents will only lead to division and stress in the family.

You may never have the same relationship with your step-grandchildren that you have with your biological grandchildren, but make the effort to get to know them and be involved in their lives.

Sara and Paul found themselves part of a blended family. They learned that planning was essential if they were to have all their grandchildren together.

They bought a cabin in the mountains and started a new tradition. On the same weekend, twice a year, they held an open house for all their family. Both the adult children and grandchildren began to appreciate the benefits of a "larger" family. The step-grandchildren soon started calling Paul and Sara, "Grandpa Paul and Grandma Sara."

The extended time and the commitment to weekends together are essential to the development of their extended family relations.

If love is what grandparenting is all about, step-grandparenting may be one of the most rewarding jobs we will ever have. Step-grandparents can be valuable role models and serve as additional caring and loving adult mentors. With understanding, time, patience and commitment, we can all learn to overcome barriers and focus on our strengths.

Jimmy, age eight, recently won his basketball championship. After the game he was asked why he was so happy. His response was, "I played well, we worked as a team and I had five grandparents here to cheer me on!"

Adoption

According to the 2000 census, three percent of the children in the United States are adopted. The following story is meant to inspire parents and grandparents to be more attune to the special needs of adopted children.

Mark woke up one morning to hear his brother singing, "Happy Birthday to Me, Happy Birthday to Daniel, Happy Birthday to Me!"

Mark had heard him sing this and it filled him with anger. Eventually his anger got the best of him and he yelled at his brother to be quiet. It didn't stop there. Mark began throwing things and proceeded to punch Daniel.

His mother heard the commotion and came running up the steps. She quickly saw and heard what Mark had done and approached his bed, "Why was I not good enough to keep?" His mother immediately understood.

Mark was an adopted Korean boy who lived with a won-

derful family, but that didn't eliminate the fact he didn't un-
derstand why he wasn't living with his birth parents. Mark's
mother assured him that his parents did not give him up be-
cause they didn't love him but, to the contrary, because they did
love him. She also assured him that both she and his father loved
him very much and would love him as long as they lived.

Mark is typical of many adopted children who, as they grow older, begin asking difficult questions about their family of origin:

- When is my real birthday?
- Did you know my "real" mother and father?
- Where are my parents today? Can I see them?
- Do my parents love me?
- Do I have other brothers and sisters? Will I ever meet them?
- Why wasn't I good enough to keep?

Questions like Mark's need be answered early and as often as necessary. Fortunately, Mark's mother provided a wonderful response when the questions were asked. How long had Mark been thinking about this before his emotional outburst?

Parents should conscientiously provide the answers and grandparents can be a big support. Adopted children will have questions that should be answered simply, accurately and with as much information as you believe the child can manage. It is also important for grandparents to tell the parents about questions and conversations they have with an adopted child and make sure that parents' and grandparents' answers are consistent with each other.

Today, Mark is a very successful young man with a bright future who will always have questions about his past. He truly celebrates his birthday every year. He has been known to sing Happy Birthday to himself!

The "sandwich" generation

Many baby boomers are being "sandwiched" between helping their children and their parents. Who should they care for today?

My eighty-six-year-old mother had been suffering for several months with a series of ailments. We observed her condition worsening and her frustration increasing. At the suggestion of her doctor, we accompanied her to a regional medical facility for a battery of tests.

Valuing the elderly

I was seated with my mother, father and sister in the doctor's office when a man entered the room eating potato chips. He was wearing slacks with a large mustard-like stain on one side. We wondered if this was really the doctor. He indicated that my sister was sitting in his chair then began abruptly to fire a series of questions and comments at my mother.

"What is it that you think we can do for you?" I don't understand why you came here. Your doctor had no business sending you here. What do you think we can possibly do for you today? We have less than an hour before the clinic closes.

What pain are you experiencing? I don't know why your doctor sent you here . . . there is nothing we can do for you. You are 86 years old. We have a number of patients in that lobby who need my attention."

Finally, I had witnessed all I could take. I interrupted the doctor:

"I fail to understand why you are being so disrespectful to my mother. My mother has been sick for three months; a physician has referred us here and all you have done is criticize her for being here. I requested that he talk with my mother, not ridicule her for seeking help.

The doctor appeared shocked, his response alarming: "We

normally don't have this number of guests in this room and if you don't control yourself, I will have security remove you from this hospital."

I knew I had to contain the anger that was rushing through me if my mother was ever to receive the care she needed.

At that moment, to my astonishment, the doctor's tone and demeanor began to change. He put his head down on his desk for a moment and began again. He proceeded to conduct a complete physical exam and called in another specialist to examine my mother.

I left the room when the second doctor entered. As the doctor walked my mother out of the room, he asked her to tell me that he was sorry for his inappropriate behavior. With proper medication her condition gradually improved.

I now understand how important it is for adult children to be attentive to their aging parents. It's critical that adult children take the lead to ensure that our parents receive the attention and respect they deserve.

Ideas & suggestions
for parents

1. Mom and Dad aren't perfect

No one is! If you've experienced conflict with your parents, what are you going to do about it? You can accept it, do nothing and things are not likely to change, or you can decide to do something to improve your relationship. Remember you are also an adult.

Consider the following:

- Visualize the relationship you would like to have with your parents
- Determine what practical steps you could take to do your part in making that relationship a reality
- Share your vision with your parents verbally or in writing
- Recognize that change will not be easy and that you are responsible only for your actions
- Be prepared to make additional changes as needed.

2. I don't approve of my child's friend. What can I do?

We choose our friends for different reasons. We want our children to make decisions for themselves. It is hard for parents to stand back and see their child being exposed to things they don't like.

I suggest that rather than disapprove of your child's friend, be sure your child is aware of the behavior his friend has displayed which causes you concern.

"Johnny was disrespectful when he lied to you yesterday."

"Mary said she would be here today and she isn't."

"Linda wants to be your friend but she didn't come to your birthday party. Have you thought about that?"

Make every effort not to nag in the process. Your task is to help your child understand specifically the behavior that concerns you. Let your child decide what to do about it. If your child has the same values you do, the child will adopt a get-tough attitude with his friend or find a new friend. Unless your child is in danger, use this opportunity to reinforce their ability to make choices. These are the choices that clarify values.

3. My parents buy extravagant gifts for our children

Many grandparents had few earthly possessions when they were young and now go overboard—buying clothes and toys. Instead, encourage your parents to invest in a college account instead of buying Barbie's latest yacht.

Assume your responsibility. Effective communication is the key to resolving any situation. Don't let your children "end-run" you to get Grandpa to buy the $200 videogame if you've already said "no." Explaining why your child can't have a videogame will help grandparents understand and help them make better choices in the future.

Ideas & suggestions
for grandparents

1. The death of a partner

Dealing with the loss of a partner, family member or friend is one of the most difficult things we must face in life. The stronger the bond you have with that individual, the longer their memory will remain with you. Everyone wants to be remembered. Don't deny his or her memory; celebrate it.

Everyone feels and handles death differently. Seek help from family and friends. On the anniversary of a loved one's death have a special service or visit the gravesite.

Time has a way of healing loss, but if you find yourself overwhelmed, it's important to seek help.

2. Defining our role in the family

Each of us has a role or a combination of roles in the family: the organizer, teacher, guide, mentor, historian, financial advisor, legal council, medical resource or spiritual leader. Use the following questions to help define your role:

- What would you like your role to be?
- Does your role support the family? In what way?
- As a member of this family, what are your responsibilities and expectations?
- What skills or abilities do you have that family members look to you for?
- Are you comfortable with your role?
- Have you communicated to your extended family that you are available to them?

- Does your role in the family include interaction with your extended family?

3. Your adult child wants to borrow money

Issues about money will be with us as long as we live. Should you help your children financially? I believe if you can, yes. However, the answer isn't quite that simple. Consider the following when giving your children financial assistance:

- Put all loans over $100 in writing. The written agreement should include interest information, the term of the loan and be signed and dated by all parties involved
- Be specific on how the money will be repaid, if it is not, what penalties will be imposed
- If the loan is sizable and not repaid, do you want to consider this in your financial will?
- Be sure the money is not money you will need short-term and that all parties clearly understand what they are signing

4. Avoid taking sides in family conflicts

Most conflict can be resolved if everyone could keep an open mind. Listening and patience are key components in keeping family together. You can't change the past, but you can make amends. Apologies and forgiveness can heal your child's or your own emotional wounds. Listen to both sides of the struggle and be sure you understand all the issues. Many times when someone is struggling with a problem, what is most needed is someone to listen, not provide solutions. Avoid taking sides, attempt to clarify the reasons for the struggle. Be prepared to provide love and comfort not only to your grandchildren, but your adult child as well.

A memory can have a lifelong impact

10

Being a family miles apart

Staying in touch

A ccording to AARP, sixty-six percent of grandparents have at least one grandchild who lives more than a day's drive away. Grandparent expert, Charmaine Ciardi, stated, "It takes more imagination and effort to grandparent long distance, but the potential for magic is still there." Much has been written about long-distance grandparenting, but as families continue to spread throughout the country and the world, the challenge to remain connected becomes even greater.

The telephone is still one of the most effective means we have of keeping in touch from a distance. A tone of voice can give more information than an e-mail. I recommend establishing a time each week to make your call. The use of calling cards, when home or abroad, helps to keep costs to a minimum. Phone cards make wonderful gifts. When you do call, ask to speak with each grandchild or one particular grandchild. Imagine the look on your grandchild's face when Mom says, "Grandpa doesn't want to talk to me, he called to talk to you!"

A fax machine or scanner is a great way for your grandchildren to send artwork. Children love drawing pictures and grandparents enjoy receiving them and putting them on display. Faxes, like phone and e-mail, are instant. In today's culture, instant is good.

Be creative and find unique ways to bridge the gap between visits. Carole Gesme, in her book, While We're Apart, offers wonderful ideas for keeping in touch with children through activities mailed back and forth between grandparents and grandchildren.

The following suggestions will not make up for the fact that you aren't physically together, but they will help in your efforts to stay connected despite the distance:

- Send tapes, recorded in your voice, reading or telling a story or talking about what you are doing.
- Send jokes and jingles.
- Send surprise packages when grandkids least expect it.
- Use video mail or video pictures of you doing ordinary things like sitting at the computer, cleaning your house or working in the garden.
- Write whenever you think about your grandchild. When they write back, keep the letters in a folder.
- Send pictures for grandkids to color and a stamped envelope for their return.
- Take a photo of their artwork on your refrigerator and send it to them.
- When traveling, send postcards of the places you visit.

- Order a magazine subscription in their name. The beauty of magazines is that they arrive regularly without your having to remember to send them.
- Go to the same movies and talk or write about what you liked or disliked.

You are a successful long-distance grandparent when your grandchildren know you care and believe they are an important part of your life.

With our children and grandchildren spread throughout the country and the world, traditional forms of communication are no longer adequate. Different time zones, cultures and languages can even make saying "hello" difficult. Yet the need to communicate and maintain family relationships is more critical than ever.

New technologies developed in the last two decades have made keeping in touch easier. Web sites and e-mail allow us to communicate with words as well as pictures, day or night, in any time zone. Whatever the form of communication, it should be ongoing as our daily lives move and change.

> **"Grandparents can suggest; the ultimate decision rests with the parents."**
> — *Grandma Group*

As a grandfather, with personal experience in long distance grandparenting, I can assure you it's not an easy task. Three of my four granddaughters live in Uppsala, Sweden. We are physically together twice a year, if we are lucky.

Recently, I had the opportunity to be with my six-year-old granddaughter. I was feeling overwhelmed. Where do I begin? It had been almost seven months since we had been together. Each time we reunite, it takes time to reestablish our relationship.

Building and rebuilding relationships with your grandchildren is similar to building any relationship. When you see someone after a long absence, there's going to be some initial discomfort. The same is true with your grandchildren; proceed cautiously, it's only natural. When reacquainting, begin slowly, be patient and watch the child's face for your next cue.

One benefit of being a long-distance grandparent is your visit is usually days not hours. Take advantage of the opportunity to "walk in their shoes." See where they play and take time to meet their friends. Attend their schools, meet their teachers and learn about what they like to do. Visiting your grandchildren at school can provide a new perspective of your grandchild in a group setting. Time in your child's environment will provide you with knowledge and information about your grandchildren as well as "points of interest" for later conversations.

Children's expectation and excitement of your long-awaited visit is a wonderful welcome. When I visit my granddaughters, the trip has usually been planned months in advance. I use this time to get reacquainted. It's fun to call, send cards and pictures and discuss our future get-together. My granddaughters always have plenty of ideas about what we can do.

Dear Grandma,

I can't wait for you to come! Mommy and Daddy are excited, too. I know because they have been talking about you coming every night at dinner. This time when you come, I hope you tell me that story again about riding a horse when you were young.

See you soon!

R.

P.S. I think my brother is excited, too.

Don't forget to plan time with your adult child. It seems obvious, but is often overlooked. Schedule time to be alone. Your adult children value and want your time and attention, too.

Continue to grow your relationships once you return home. What you do between visits is as important as the visit itself. Children love to see pictures of themselves again and again. A digital camera provides you an easy way to share pictures quickly to an infinite number of people. Besides paper prints, which can be mailed, you can have your photos transferred to a CD and send photos with e-mail. There are a number of Internet sites where you can download pictures from a digital camera and share them immediately. The following are three of the most popular sites:

www.comstock.com
www.shutterfly.com
www.snapfish.com

Traveling with your grandchildren

Research completed by American Demographics found that a growing number of intergenerational families plan to travel together. The same study found that children (ages six to seventeen) would like a vacation with their grandparents.

More than ever before, grandparents are choosing to take their grandchildren with them on trips. According to Vern Bengston, a gerontology professor at University of Southern California, "Vacations are one of the biggest ways grandparents are influencing, nurturing and helping to raise grandchildren today."

Participants in Grandkidsandme programs are usually equally split between grandpas and grandmas, though mothers and grandmothers do the majority of the planning. Many mothers and grandmothers, particularly with granddaughters, request time for grandfathers to be with their grandchildren.

Victor Zullo, author of The Nanas and Papas, supports grandparents traveling with their grandchildren, "They want to buy them experiences that they can do together."

If you are traveling to a U.S. National park, consider purchasing the Golden Age Passport. The Passport is available to U.S. citizens or permanent residents who are age 62 or older as well as citizens who have a permanent disability. There is a one-time charge of $10, and the pass is good for life. The passport provides free entrance to most federal recreation areas and provides a 50% discount on user fees. Golden Age Passports are available at national parks or federal recreation areas. More information can be obtained at www.us-parks.com or any national park.

Many businesses and non-profits have picked up on the trend of grandparent participation in travel. Elderhostel, a non-profit that combines international travel packages with liberal arts study programs for people of retirement age, offers over 100 intergenerational and grandparent programs in the U.S. Grandtravel, www.grandtrvl.com provides international and domestic travel packages for grandchildren to more than twenty destinations designed specifically for grandparents and their grandchildren.

Other web sites offering various grandparent travel information include:

Grandma Betty www.grandmabetty.com
Grandparent World www.grandparentworld.com
Senior Women's Travel www.poshnosh.com

Survival tips for traveling with grandchildren

1. Gain support and permission
When parents support travel plans, most problems will be overcome before you start. If you don't have the support of both parents, don't go!

2. I'm scared!

It's not unusual for young children to be afraid to stay with their grandparents. If you don't see each other often, spend time getting to know one another before your trip. Consider taking older brothers or sisters along until the grandchild is comfortable.

3. Plan early

Plan early and get parents and grandchildren involved. Depending on the length of the trip and travel arrangements, it's a good rule of thumb to begin several months in advance. Plan together and share all information as it gathered. If your grandchild uses the Internet, send links or mail pictures of what you intend to see.

4. Rest time

More trips are ruined because of lack of proper rest than for any other reason. It's a good idea to plan for one day of rest for every three days of travel. Don't forget time zone changes.

5. Record what's going on

Write down things you see and discuss them with parents and grandchildren before, during and after your trip. Encourage everyone to journal each day. Pictures, pictures and more pictures are, of course, great. Children love taking their own pictures and with inexpensive disposable cameras, there is little reason for the grandchildren to not have their own camera. If you have a digital camera, send pictures immediately when you return. Have pictures made into postcards or t-shirts after the trip as a memento of your fun together.

6. Take along stuff

Things from home can be very comforting on a long trip. If the child has a favorite teddy bear, doll, or blanket, don't hesitate to bring it along. Imaginary friends are welcome as well. They take up little space and don't have luggage.

My granddaughter took along a picture of mom and dad and her sisters on a recent trip. Each night before she went to bed, she talked to them.

7. Plan for the unexpected

Remember the obvious; phone numbers, first aid kit, medications, sunscreen and bug spray.

In case of emergency, always have a medical treatment slip signed by both parents along with necessary insurance information. On the permission slip state plainly the purpose of your trip, the dates of the trip and who has temporary custody of the child. Consider this a requirement if you are traveling out of the country. Depending on the country, border guards may require it.

8. Preventative measures

Know your grandchild's habits and special needs such as when they usually get up, eat, take naps and go to bed. Know too what your grandchild may be afraid of and how to best provide comfort.
Discuss with the parents any other unique behaviors you might not be aware of.

9. Plan for sudden changes in weather

Depending on where you are planning to go or the time of year; bring along an umbrella, extra jackets or sweatshirts and a change of shoes.

Grandchildren are children—not angels

Children or grandchildren can indeed disrupt our lives. They are supposed to. A grandchild around the house means handprints on the walls, more dishes in the sink, larger grocery bills, more garbage, more meals, spills, noise, laundry, being tired and little private time. Fortunately, it also means more smiles, excitement in the morning, questions all day, an opportunity for you to grow, someone on your lap and lots of kisses.

Being a successful grandparent requires you to accept discomfort, aggravation and frustration peppered with comfort, joy and love.

A grandparents' wish list

I hope you will go fishing with me. Better yet, I hope you clean the fish and learn how to properly dispose of the remains.

I hope I can teach you how to make chocolate chip cookies and Rice Crispy treats and experience the pleasure of licking the spatula when we're done.

I hope we can take long walks together, and learn that the value is not solely for our bodies, but our minds.

I hope you feel cared for and the love of family and friends.

I hope you learn from your dog what unconditional love is.

I hope the batteries in your electronic games continue to "run out" and that you find time to play a game of hide and seek with your brother, sister and cousins.

I hope you don't get a college scholarship and that you work during and after college to pay your tuition.

I hope you learn to laugh at, and learn from, your mistakes.

I hope that your degree doesn't automatically provide you with $60,000 a year job, but instead you work in less than ideal conditions with a demanding boss.

I hope you learn to appreciate an old apartment with too many roommates and no air conditioning.

I hope that you will find enough time to do all the fun things you want to do.

I hope you don't have a new car to drive on a long trip, but instead go on a crowded bus with a very diverse group of people.

I hope you never have so much of anything that you don't need to ask your neighbor for help.

I hope you have credit card payments that force you to make tough decisions.

I hope you find comfort and security in your own home.

I hope you always have time to read a good book.

I hope that you witness the marvels of nature: butterflies dancing on the wind, deer running in the woods, birds flying south and the shadows of trees in the autumn forest.

I hope you learn that the "other guy" always wins the lottery.

I hope you remember to share what you have with those less fortunate.

I hope your children won't learn everything the first time and they are forced to ask for help.

And finally, at the end of each day, when you count your blessings, I hope you remember to be thankful for the trials, tribulations and challenges that provided you with your wisdom.

Ideas & suggestions
for parents
& grandparents

1. Communicating with infants

Begin communication when your grandchild is born. This may not be possible when step-grandchildren join the family. The sound of your voice and the impressions you leave will form the foundation for your relationship.

If you can't be there in person, begin by talking on the phone with your grandchildren when they are as young as a few months. Share the same things you would say if you were holding them in your arms. Sing songs or tell a story. End by telling your children you love them.

2. Friends are important, especially to teenagers

When a child is a teenager, friends are the most important relationships in their life. Teenagers prefer to talk to, confide in and share feelings with their friends. How you accept these friends and incorporate them into your family will go a long way as to how you will relate to your teenager. In order to maintain and grow your communication, you need to try to understand the teenage world. Express to your teenage grandchild that you want to be a part of their lives.

Share your own struggles for independence and identity. I suspect there will be some good material for laughter as you reflect on your tales from the past.

Talk with your grandchildren and learn how they think about the following:

- Your friends are important to you, why?
- How are you and your friends alike?
- How are your friends different from you?
- Do you have enough time for yourself?
- Where do you like to spend time?
- What would you like us to do together?
- What do you want our relationship to be?

3. What are your grandchild's fears?

We cannot eliminate fear but we can provide a secure, comfortable place to talk about it. Whenever you have the opportunity, help your grandchildren identify and overcome their fears.

I caution you not to dismiss your grandchild's fears. They are real and deserve your attention. Common fears of children:

- Being "different" from other kids
- No one likes them
- Moving or changing schools
- Physical harm
- Losing someone they love
- Fear of the dark
- Parents will divorce
- Parents might get sick or die

4. Junk bag for happy traveling

Bring along stuff, that you and your child or grandchild might do while traveling; books, travel games and cards. Don't forget items for yourself.

Depending on the age of your grandchildren, bring along a Junk Bag." In it's place items you might use at a roadside stop such as a sand shovel and pail, a couple of trucks, a Frisbee, and a ball.

Healthy, non-messy food snacks for those numerous occasions when hunger strikes are always a good idea and saves on the wallet as well.

A special treat on our trips is crackers and squirt cheese.

5. The trip plan with your grandchild

If you know the route, draw a map or start a scrapbook of things you might watch for along the way. Leave a copy of the route and times when you expect to be at any given location with parents.

How many times have we all heard, hen are we going to get there? Plan frequent stops; snacks, meals, visits to historical markers, a game of catch, bathroom breaks, or just to look at things of interest.

Plan, too, for things you would like to share about yourself with your grandchildren. Share some of their favorite childhood stories. Write down the questions you might ask before you go:

- Who is your favorite friend and why?
- If you could have three wishes, what would you wish for?
- What animal reminds you most of yourself?
- What animal reminds you most of me?
- What animal is your favorite and why?

Being together

11

History, ancestors and preserving our heritage

Recording family history

A long-standing traditional role of grandparents has been to maintain records of family history. Our ancestors knew that one of the keys to understanding themselves was to look at their roots. We appear to have an innate desire to know our ancestry. Recently at a family reunion, I was amazed to see family members, young and old, search a four-foot by thirty-foot chart of our family tree for their ancestors.

My ninety-seven-year-old aunt was my inspiration to probe into my family history. She kept disorganized scraps of history and collected newspaper clippings. She also told wonderful stories.

An important link to the past can be lost forever when a generation dies. Historical records provide some information but the "real stories" come from older living family members and their account of the events that occurred.

I encourage you to examine your own family history. What you do without expected return will bring you unexpected results. Talk to the elder members of your family, record their stories and share them with your children and grandchildren. Families enjoy hearing the stories and learning about the personal sacrifices our ancestors endured on our behalf.

> "Your kids have taken the very best of you, improved on it and are passing that on to your grandchildren."
> — Judy Ford, Author of
> *Wonderful Ways to Love a Grandchild*

The record keeping of each subsequent generation has become more complex through multiple marriages, divorce and adoption. "A salad bowl" has replaced the family tree.

Your story, an ethical will

An ethical will is the story or mini-biography of your life and the values and legacy you hope will be remembered. Just as a financial will tells the story of your finances, an ethical will tells the story of one's life. Ethical wills can include valuable family historical information.

Ethical wills go back to the time of the Bible. According to Barry Baines, an expert on ethical wills, the first ethical will can be found in the Bible, Genesis, Chapter 49. Not only were the names and descendants recorded here, but their stories. For generations there have been pages in bibles designed specifically to record family history.

Historical stories of our family have great value and provide another key to who you are. Our forefathers and mothers created their own paths. They traveled across oceans, built homes in a new country far from family, learned a new language, dealt with plagues and fought in wars.

I predict that in the near future, our life's history will be stored on family web sites that will not only record the stories of our ancestors but will provide the family with an ongoing "newspaper" of family events through pictures and written information. It will be history in progress. I would strongly encourage you to begin writing your ethical will.

Writing your ethical will

Writing an ethical will is the process of looking at your life and answering some important questions such as: who you are, where you have come from, where you want to go with the remainder of your life, what you value, what you hope to leave for the next generation and how you would like to be remembered.

The process of writing your ethical will can help you clarify your role in the family, values and what you believe is important for future generations. Recording more of each respective generation's story can be of great assistance to the next generation in developing their story. An ethical will is your personal story and history recorded for posterity.

An ethical will is as important as your financial will and can have more impact on the people you care about. Your story is likely to become clearer as the secrets of your life are revealed. Be patient with yourself, it takes time before real clarity can occur. Update your ethical will as events dictate.

The following questions will assist you in getting started:

- What are the values I want to pass on to my children and grandchildren?
- Who were the mentors in my life?

- What personal stories would I like to share?
- What do I consider my real accomplishments?
- What are my disappointments?
- What stories do I remember about my parents and relatives?
- What are my strong beliefs and where did they come from?
- What lessons have I learned?
- What events changed my life?
- How would I like to be remembered?

Ethical wills can be recorded in one or more of the following ways: computer, paper, tape or video. Some people attach their ethical will to their financial will. Others record it, save it on a CD and give it to their children on a special occasion. Others store the recording in a safe or safety deposit box to be read at the time of death.

Some of us go through life without a clear roadmap of where we are going. We let life happen to us instead of planning. An ethical will can be a roadmap to where we want to go from here.

My ancestors are me

I am not alone
I walk this earth with their memories and their strength
Decisions in life can be lonely when you feel alone
My decisions do not need to be mine alone
I am not alone
I walk this earth with their memories
Their memories have become me

My Dad, the pilot

The following story is excerpted from Don's ethical will.

My 85-year-old Father grew up on the family farm in southern Minnesota and became the third generation of Schmitz's to farm the land. It's been in the Schmitz name for over 130 years.

In his early 30's, Dad and his brother-in-law, Joe, decided to take flying lessons. They took a couple of lessons, loved it and soon decided to buy an old Aeronca airplane. Dad built a hanger and a landing strip in the nearby hayfield.

Dad's favorite tale was about his sister-in-law, Lorraine. It was a nice, warm day and Dad had flown the plane to his father-in-law's house. He drove the plane up to the farm buildings and went into the house for dinner. Unbeknownst to him, while he was eating, one of his nephews had climbed into the plane and moved the controls.

After dinner, Lorraine decided she wanted to go flying. My father tried to talk her out of it, but she insisted. Dad helped Lorraine crawl into the back of the airplane as the entire family watched with anticipation. He cranked the propeller and much to everyone's surprise, the plane suddenly started down the field. Dad and my uncle Fran chased after it. Dad was able to grab one of the wings and force the plane into a circle, reach inside and pull down the throttle to stop the plane. It had been pushed wide open for take off!

Lorraine decided on the spot her flying days were over but Dad flew for several more years and had many memorable adventures. Dad's flying career ended the day the pigs escaped from their pen and chewed out the bottom of the plane.

Today, I have trouble picturing my father as a pilot, but this was one of the proudest times in my father's life. Flying an airplane made him different from his father, who had seen the land from the ground only.

Next month Jessie, my niece will be soloing. So, where did Jessie get the idea to be a pilot?

Shared passions and values

Ideas & suggestions
for parents

1. A story from the past

Recall your life stories and identify the components of your values. Write down twenty-five words or phrases that describe your childhood. For example: baseball, gravel-roads, movies, snowstorms, cabin, morning, carnival, corn, earth, singing, doctors, corner store, wringer-washer, soap, candy, horses, buses, chalk, buried, polkas, storms, bedroom, recess.

Now arrange the words into sentences that tell the stories of your childhood.

2. Why we do the things we do?

Over the course of our lives, we make decisions about what we like and dislike. Have you ever wondered why? Answers to these questions can help us learn more about ourselves and provide clarity about what we want to impart to our children. The following questions can guide your investigation:

- Do you like to read, learn and listen to music?
- How did you decide on your career?
- What are your interests?
- Who or what were the influences in your life?
- How did your interests develop?

Ideas & suggestions
for grandparents

1. The ancestry treasure chest

Photographs, letters, documents, certificates, medals, awards, newspaper clippings, report cards and copies of public records are all important personal effects to assist you in developing your ancestry treasure chest. Interviews are the best method of gathering your "treasure chest" of family history. Interview all living members of your family tree:

- What important historical pieces of family information do you know? Where did the information come from?
- What stories would you like your grandchildren to know?
- Describe your childhood house and neighborhood.
- How old were you when you got married?
- Where did you get married?
- How old were you when you had your first child?
- How old were you when you became grandparents?
- Who was your best friend?
- Where did you go to school?
- How did your family make a living?
- What activities did you do with your parents?
- What special talents did your parents have?
- How many brothers and sisters did you have?
- How did you like being a parent?
- In what way are you like your parents?

2. Creating your future

Do you lack a compelling vision for what is next in your life? Government has identified the age of sixty-five for retirement. Our society frequently interprets this to mean, No more plans. Is this true for you?

At sixty-five, we have approximately one-fourth of our life left to live. Planning can make our retirement life full and exciting. Inventory your time and resources now. What is possible?

- What is your plan today for the rest of your life?
- Is your life what you want it to be?
- Is your family a part of your plan?
- Is it time to return to school?
- Is it time to resurface old dreams never realized?
- Do you resist change?
- With whom will you share your plan?

Society and ideally you, yourself, have given you permission to do whatever you want.

3. Great-grandparenting

Today, with grandparents and great grandparents living into there eighties and nineties, there is an ever-growing population who has a wealth of experience and wisdom but few role models to guide the way.

The following questions can assist you in developing your vision of great-grandparenting:

- At what age are you likely to be a great-grandparent?
- How will you relate to a much younger generation?

- What experiences have you had, if shared, would enhance a young life?
- How will your role be different from your role as a grandparent?
- How do you want to be remembered?

4. Encourage tradition

Traditions we establish with family are important. They are meaningful and support relationships among people of every age. Try new things. When something works; do it every year. You will soon have a meaningful tradition of your own. It is never too late to begin a new tradition:

- Celebrate all birthdays at one time; create a universal birthday party.
- Prepare favorite recipes together.
- Hold a summer family picnic that occurs the same weekend every year.
- Arrange a family garden tour.
- Begin a family conference call on the second Sunday of every month.
- At holiday time: decorate a Christmas tree together, light an advent wreath, write holiday greeting cards or host a Chanukah Party .

Adventures together can be lots of fun

The lake, the woods, fresh air, bright stars; that's camp

12

Pass it on

"Tell your children of it,
and let your children tell their children
another generation."

— Joel 1:3

Tell stories

One benefit of getting older is recalling the antics and stories of your children when they were young. Everyone likes to hear stories about their childhood and who has more stories or can remember them better than their parents?

Grandparents have the gift of longevity and in the best position to share stories of their adult children. Grandchildren love to hear stories about their parents when they were children and your adult children like to be reminded of who they once were. As your grandchildren grow older, they too will want to hear stories about themselves, even though their stories are very recent history.

The Chicken Man

This is a true story from my childhood. I have told this story dozens of times. Now I share this story with my grandchildren. They always say, "Tell us that chicken story again!"

A sure sign of spring on the Schmitz family farm was the arrival of five hundred baby chicks. Every year the chicks were delivered around Easter. Along with their arrival came a whole new year of chicken experiences.

Because my father liked the cows, he spent most of his work-day caring for the cows. My older brother liked working with the pigs. Since I was next in line, my job by default was to care for the chickens. It wasn't my first choice, but someone had to do it. At some point, I grew to appreciate chickens and I think they appreciated me.

When the chicks were about three months old, we would catch each of the five hundred chicks, one by one. We used flash-lights to spot the chickens perched in the trees. Climbing the trees and grabbing the chickens while they were sleeping was great fun. After they were captured, Dad or Mom would put little metal glasses on their beaks. Putting glasses on chickens doesn't hurt them and it stops the chickens from pecking and hurting each other. With glasses, chickens can't look straight ahead; they look on both sides instead.

The entire family would get involved: my two brothers, four sisters, mom and dad. It was a big job putting glasses on chickens but the fun was doing it as a family. It was an annual event, we all, including myself the chicken man, looked forward to each year.

In telling stories of our childhood, we entertain not only our children and grandchildren, but also gain insight into how we became who we are today. A story from our childhood will remind us of how we felt as a child and help us to remember the importance of family in our lives.

Unconditional love, reindeers, & that guy named Santa

When I was a young boy on a farm in Southern Minnesota, I recall walking to the barn, looking up at the Milky Way and being captivated for the longest time because I saw "Him." I saw Santa and his reindeer!

One evening, I told my older brother and sister what I had seen, and you know their response? "Oh, Don, you are such a dreamer!" To this day, I know I really did see that round little man.

It was a great disappointment to me when I was forced to face reality. The feeling of disappointment remained with me for years. I wanted to believe so much in Santa and what he stood for. Santa was the greatest! He showered everyone with unconditional gifts.

When I was a teenager, my uncle asked me if I would be Santa for his children. I was elated. It was a memorable experience. I saw the look in my young cousins' eyes and recognized those feelings from long ago.

As I drove home that night, I looked up at the star-filled sky. What I saw, I will never forget. My spirit was touched in a special way. I realized I wasn't just dressing up like Santa; I was Santa and all he represents. On that night, that spirit became a part of me.

The holiday season is a time for all of us to dress up and be Santa to all those in need. Unfortunately, this simple lesson can be understood only as we mature. Our unconditional love is really a gift to ourselves.

So, did I really see Santa that night? I know the answer.

Grandparents indeed can be historians and the guardians of great treasures of family history.

Grandma isn't too bright, or is she?

Mary loved to help her grandma make chocolate chip cookies. Her job was to put the chocolate chips in the cookies.

When Mary was about eight years old, Grandma asked Mary for a special favor. "Mary, do you know what two-thirds of a cup of flour is?" Mary looked at her grandmother in a curious way and said, "Sure, I know what two-thirds of a cup is!" Grandma said with a smile, "I am so glad you came to help me; how could I make cookies without you?

Mary thought to herself after, Grandma had gone to school for only eight grades, so maybe she never learned what two-thirds of a cup was.

From that day on, Mary did the measuring of the flour, because Grandma didn't "seem" to know how to do it. Now, Mary had two jobs she could help her Grandma with and that made her feel all the more important!

Many years later, when Mary was in high school, she understood what Grandma had done for her.

Music and song connect

Music has a way of touching

"Songs can sometimes do what spoken words can't."

Leroy Vague, our resident guitarist at Grandparent Camp, wrote the following song. The song is a wonderful story about a father watching his son in his grandfather's arms. His son squirms and wiggles and finally settles on a special place on his grandfather's chest.

The song speaks to the importance of physical touch and the comfort that it alone can provide.

Lay Your Head Where My Heart Is

Verse 1
I would always enjoy watching my little boy
As he climbed on grandpa's chair
It was time for a nap, so he'd sit on his lap
While grandpa sang that simple prayer:

Chorus
Lay your head where my heart is
Close your eyes dear little child
Lay your head where my heart is
Let it rest there for a while

Verse 2
It wouldn't take long listening to that song
And before I count to ten
His eyes begin to close and he'd begin to doze
While Grandpa sang those words once again:

Verse 3
It was meant for my son
and when that song was done
My cares drifted away and the thought came to me
How lucky we would be if we all had someone to say:

Chorus repeated

Lay your head where my heart is
Close your eyes dear little child
Lay your head where my heart is
Let it rest there for a while

Books are valuable tools

Reading to your grandchildren is one of the most fulfilling times you can experience. When your grandchild snuggles close to you or climbs on your lap, there is a feeling that is difficult to capture with words. The warmth registers deep into your soul.

Countless children's books provide you with a wonderful vehicle to give the gift of you to your grandchildren.

A friend of mine takes a book to her grandchildren each time she visits. As soon as she arrives, she gives her grandchildren a book and immediately, they are off to examine the contents. It isn't too long before they're back asking Grandma if she will read it to them.

Every teacher knows, even the most hyperactive child, will sit still and listen when they get caught up in the wonderful world of storybooks. I encourage you to create a library in your home in a welcoming spot for your grandchildren and regularly promote the use of its contents.

There are countless reasons for reading to children and to grandchildren:

- Books provide an opportunity for physical downtime and closeness.
- They stimulate children's imagination.
- Books create interest and excitement.
- Reading books to children is of the best methods to teach children to read.
- Books broaden knowledge and understanding.
- Books prompt conversation and questions.
- Books explore new places.
- Reading is the gift of your time and sends this message, "You are important to me."

Story time is their time

Let your grandchild select the book, even when it's the one you have read thirty times. Find a cuddly, cozy spot and enjoy the warm feeling of being physically close. Don't let anyone interfere with this precious time. Spend as much time on the pictures as the words.

With books, children acquire new knowledge and an opportunity to share what they know. Share your own experiences when you can. Reading all the words is optional. The children often know the story word for word, so change the

> "My grandchildren help me give myself away and in the process, I discover myself. "
> — *Grandparent group*

story a bit, to make it more fun. Ask questions to keep their attention. Personalize the tale by using the children's names, when possible. Start the sentence and let your grandchildren finish. Let your grandchild hold the book and turn the pages.

When children become proficient in reading, switch roles. Let the child do the reading and you become the active listener. Active listeners ask open-ended questions. Have fun and become the role model of an active listener.

When I haven't seen my grandchildren for a period of time, a book is the best way to rekindle our relationship. On a recent trip to Sweden, my youngest granddaughter wanted little to do with me until her older sisters pulled out a book. Soon she was curled up beside me, listening to every word and completely unaware of how close she was sitting to me.

Children love repetition. Repetition provides practice developing the prerequisite skills necessary to further develop their language. Be enthusiastic and use a variety of voice tones. Give the characters voices, then let the children be the voices.

Incorporate the story into their lives throughout the day. Most stories have a moral that can be applied to our lives.

As you read to your grandchildren, experience the joy of being a grandparent and breathe it deep into your soul.

The "Grandparent Gold Mine"

A "Grandparent Gold Mine" is a special place where grandchildren go to experiment and explore. Grandparents should have a Grandparent Gold Mine in their bag of tricks. The "Gold Mine" has unlimited possibilities. The contents should encourage experimentation, be fun, spark curiosity and be safe.

To find the contents for your gold mine, go to garage sales and look for the unusual. Think like a child, if you see something and wonder what it is, it's probably a slam-dunk for your Grandparent Gold Mine.

Many materials can be used to build things and others just to inspire. The following items are possible treasures you might want to include in your Gold Mine:

pictures & magazines	paints
wood blocks	snake skins
nuts & bolts	grandma's perfume
picture postcards	fishing lures, feathers, & furs
magic markers	needle & thread
ribbon & rope	packing material
pieces of metal	old hats & clothes
glue & glitter	jewelry
cardboard	screws & nails
wrapping paper	rubber stamps
magnets	rock collections
boxes & bones	

Once you've collected the items, arrange them in boxes, cans or envelopes. Organizing your treasures will make it easier to bring out a group of interesting materials that aren't overwhelming. Old dressers or large boxes, make great places for Gold Mines to be stored.

Once the grandchildren come for a visit, pull out a drawer or box and explore.

Think about what might spark children's interest and encourage them to ask questions. It won't take long for you to learn each grandchild's favorite drawer. Keep the drawers refreshed as supplies run out and enjoy the fun.

Gifts and grandkids

"Grandchildren love gifts, but they have everything! They have so much 'stuff,' how will I know it will be appreciated?"

The next time you want to give a gift, consider giving a piece of yourself. Gifts that represent or share a piece of you will be treasured, won't break the bank and provide an opportunity to pass on a piece of your history.

Gifts that continue to grow:

1. Remembering those who came before us
Make copies of your parent's photos. Write a brief paragraph about a strength or talent that each person possesses. Place the story and the photo in a frame.

2. Unpack your bags

Give something that belongs to you: a quilt you sewed, a thimble used for knitting, a favorite fishing lure, a tool from your workshop, a dish from your mother, a story you wrote, an old report card or a piece of jewelry.

3. Make connections

Your time is a precious gift. Plan to spend time with the family throughout the year. Have a party at your home or schedule a lunch together. If you can't be together physically, find other ways. Phone calls, cards and letters are always appreciated. E-mail correspondence can be as rewarding as it is fast.

Shared experiences build relationships

Grandpa Don was not a "lemon!"

Recently, my friend Don passed away. He had been stricken with polio at the age of twelve but never stopped fighting. Don was a wonderful father and grandfather. He fought harder than most to discover and utilize his gifts.

Two weeks before Don died, the two of us were talking about business on the phone. As we were talking, he suddenly stopped me and said he had to go to his grandson's birthday party. Jokingly, I asked, "What is more important, business or your grandson? He laughed and hung up the phone.

Don's son presented the eulogy at his father's funeral. He described his father as having a "lemon of a body." The reaction by the congregation was just as Don would have want; we laughed!

Polio had destroyed the muscles throughout his body and during his teenage years Don struggled to regain the use of his arms and legs. Don loved a challenge and when he was told he would never walk, he took up the challenge. Many years and operations later, with the help of braces on his arms and legs, he walked and even played golf.

During rehabilitation, Don learned to play the guitar. He taught his children and grandchildren the love of music and the value of humor. I witnessed his influence the day of his funeral when his children and grandchildren sang songs and played their instruments.

Ideas & suggestions
for parents

1. Extended family

Extended family can provide loving mentors and friends for your children. Some ideas on building your extended family:

- Do you make an effort to involve your extended family in your family?
- Do you go on vacations together?
- Do you include your aunts and uncles in family celebrations?
- Do you remember extended family in small ways with birthday cards, emails or pictures of your family?

2. Take charge of your health

By the year 2030, forty-nine percent of our population will be over fifty-five. Will you be one of them?

- As our population continues to grey, how will this affect your life?
- What will you do today to ensure a long healthy life for yourself?
- Are there aspects of your life you can change today?
- Are you prepared to make those changes?

How would poor health affect your spouse, your children and grandchildren?

Ideas & suggestions
for grandparents

1. Stories your grandchildren would love to hear

Young children enjoy hearing about the "good old days." It is not only fun but also educational. Grandchildren would love to hear about:

- Your first car and how old you were when you started to drive.
- Ways you have actions or movements like any of your ancestors.
- Where you went on trips.
- Where you were born.
- What your mother, father, grandma and grandpa were like.
- What games you liked to play as a child.
- Your favorite books.
- What toys you remember.
- Your best friend.

2. Support your grandchildren's dreams

Nourish the dreams of your grandchildren. Grandchildren have dreams at all ages. Take time to sit down and discover what they are. Help your grandchildren believe they can accomplish whatever they set their minds to do. Let your children know you believe in them and that you are available to help.

Final Thoughts

When grandparents love again

They hold their grandchild's hand in their hands and say,
"How beautiful!"
The beating of their heart is strong with the pride in
Littleness: the nose, eyes, toes and fingers.
When they hold hands, they know;
"I am holding a piece of me."

When grandparents love again
They are reminded of "days gone by."
Their smile contains wrinkles of the wisdom of times:
When they were caressed, hugged, ignored, fought and cried.
They look at children and say,
"I want more for my grandchildren."

When grandparents love again
They share their stories with more than words.
Their faces dance, they speak softly and the
Listeners become motionless
As they are taken back to a time of
Days long since passed and a future not yet visited.

When grandparents love again
Freedom is reborn.
Limitless possibilities become everyday occurrences of
"When anything is possible."

Infant wisdom

As the family sat down to dinner; Josephine had been pondering an important question for her Dad.

"Dad, can you show me your muscles?" Dad proudly pulled up his sleeve and showed her his bicep. "What do you think?" he asked.

Josephine was mildly impressed but Dad could tell she had something else on her mind. Dad asked, "What are you thinking, Josephine?"

She answered, "Well, my friend Tobias says his Grandpa is really strong. Tobias says he can fight off crooks and bad guys."

Mom replied, "Daddy's pretty strong, too. Don't you think he could fight off crooks and bad guys, too?"

A prayer for parents and grandparents

May you have
Wisdom
Love
Peace
Health
Grounded-ness
Gentle reminders of the brevity of life
Reason to value each day
A feeling of immortality
Children and grandchildren who mirror your dreams
An understanding of your own childhood
And a desire and appreciation for each new day

A face captures time

Making time to be together

Glossary

Boomer
People born between the years 1945–1963.

Blended Family
A family made up of a minimum of two children who are not biologically related.

Bullying
Bullying is a conscious, willful and deliberate hostile action intended to instill harm.

Care-giving grandparent
A grandparent that has full responsibility for the child for a minimum of six months.

Ethical will
A story or mini-biography about your life; the values and legacy you want to pass on to subsequent generations.

Family
The U.S. Census Bureau defines a family as "a group of two or more people related by blood, marriage or adoption."

Favoritism
The disposition to favor and promote the interest of one person or family over others.

Grandparent Gold Mine
A special space created by grandparents where grandchildren can go to experiment and explore.

Grand-relations
The process of involving grandparents and great grandparents in the family unit.

Mentor
Someone who willingly shares, teaches, supports, inspires and provides direction for another person.

Salad bowl
An analogy used to describe the diverse and complex makeup of today's families.

Self-love
Learning the love of self through the caring, support of another.

Witness
People who help others celebrate important events in their life.

The research process

Parent, Grandma and Grandpa groups

In preparation for writing *The New Face of Grandparenting*, research was conducted with three groups referred to as the "Grandma Group" The "Grandpa Group" and The "Parent Group."

Questions were presented to all three groups and data was compiled. Both oral and written responses were gathered and recorded.

Because of the relatively small number of participants, no percentages were established. A consensus was reached on key points and comments of the participants were recorded.

The Parent group

The parents were an equal number of men and women between the ages of twenty-three and forty-one. Each parent had between one and four children and represented a cross section of working and stay at home parents.

Grandma and Grandpa groups

The grandparents each had between one and nine grandchildren. Two of the grandparents had step-grandchildren. For the purpose of this study it was assumed that grandchildren and step-grandchildren were the same.

The grandparents were of a similar age and ranged between fifty-one and sixty-seven years old. Some grandparents consider themselves boomer grandparents. None of the grandparents were currently care-giving grandparents though two grandparents had over the years assumed this role.

Grandparents and parents were promised anonymity. It was agreed that their specific names would not be used.

The research process

The research was conducted in the winter and spring of 2002. Each group received a list of questions one week prior to the scheduled meetings. Participants were encouraged to use e-mail and to return their responses two days prior to the meeting.

Three follow-up meetings were held every two weeks over a six-week period to discuss results. Each of the grandparent groups met separately, by gender, to review the results. Parents met as a group.

References

AARP. (January 4, 2000). AARP Survey: Grandparents, grandchildren have strong bond, visit often. [Online] Available: www.aarp.org [March 2000].

Arkins, A. (2003). Website provides "matchmaking" home-share services for single moms nationwide. [Online] Available: www.co-abode.com/press/pressrelease.php [June 10, 2003].

Bly, S. (1993). Once a parent always a parent. Wheaton IL: Tyndale House Publishers.

Baines, B. (1998). The ethical will resource kit [Brochure]. Minneapolis, MN: Josaba Ltd.

Bennis, W. & Thomas, R. (2002). Geeks & Geezers: How era, values and defining moments shape leaders. Boston, MA: Harvard Business School Publishing.

Carson, L. (1996). The essential grandparent: a guide to making a difference. Deerfield Beach, FL: Health Communications.

Campbell, R., & Chapman, G. (1999). Parenting your adult child. Chicago: Northfield Publishing.

Colorosso, B. (2003). The bully, the bullied, and the bystander: breaking the cycle of violence. Canada: Beginning Press.

Ciardi, C., & Oirme, C. (1995). The magic of grandparenting. New York: Henry Holt and Company.

Clarke, J. I., (1978). Self-esteem: a family affair. New York: Harper & Row, Publishers.

Condon, G., & Condon, J. (1995). Beyond the grave: the right way and the wrong way of leaving money to your children (and others). New York: Harper Collins.

Dalton, R., & Dalton, P. (1990). The encyclopedia of grandparenting: hundreds of ideas to entertain your grandchildren. Leandro, CA: Bristol Publishing.

Denenburg, B. (1991). Nelson Mandela: no easy walk to freedom. New York: Scholastic.

Doherty, W., & Carlson, B. (2002). Putting family first: successful strategies for reclaiming family life in a hurry-up world. Owl Books.

Elkind, D. (1990). Grandparenting/understanding today's children. Glenview, IL: Scott Foresman and Company.

Endicott, I. (1997). Grandparenting: it's not what it used to be. Nashville, Tennessee: Broadman & Holman Publishers.

Ford, J. (1997). Wonderful ways to love a grandchild. Berkeley, California: Conari Press.

Frain, B., & Clegg E. (1997). Wise parent for your grown child. Oakland, CA: New Harbinger Publications, Inc.

Gambone, J. (1998). All are welcome. Orono, MN: Elder Eye Press.

Gambone, J. (2000). Refirement: a boomers guide to life after 50. Minneapolis, MN: Kirkhouse Publishers.

Gerber, J., Wolf, J., Klores, W., & Brown, G., (1989). Life trends. New York: Macmillan Publishing Company.

Greenspan, S. (2002). The four-thirds solution. Cambridge, MS: Perseus Publishing.

Harris, B. (2003). Having a Grand(Parent) Vacation. [Online] Available: www.latimes.com [April 8, 2003].

Hofferth, S. (1999). Changes in American children's time, 1981-1997. University of Michigan's Institute of Social Research, Center Survey,

Jones, J. (1995). In the middle of the road we call life. San Francisco: Harper.

Kandell, S. (1995). Grandparent's tales: Stories our children need to hear. Doctorate dissertation, Union Institute Graduate School.

Kornhaber, A. (1996). Contemporary grandparenting. New York: Random House.

Kornhaber, A. (2002). The grandparent guide. Contemporary Books: McGraw Hill.

LaShan, E. (1993). Grandparents in a changing world. New York: Newmarket Press.

Maisel, R. (2001). All grown up: living happily ever after with your adult children. Canada: New Society Publishers.

Plunkett, S. (2003).Grandtimes. [Online] Available: www.grandtimes.com/step.html [March 1, 2003].

Quadagno, J. (1999). Aging and the life course. Boston: McGraw- Hill College.

Quatrano, C. (1995). The magic of grandparenting. New York: Henry Holt and Company.

Raynor, D. (1977). Grandparents around the world. Canada: George M. McLead Ltd.

Sanders, B. (2003). Childcare in America. [Online]. www.bernie.house.gov/statements/20020401124809.asp [April 1, 2002].

Schmitz, D. (1998). A review of coaching change. Independent Study Contract I, St. Mary's Human Development Program, Minneapolis, MN.

Schmitz, D. (1999). Grandparenthood; legacy and heritage. Independent study contract III, St. Mary's Human Development Program, Minneapolis, MN.

Shalomi, Z., & Miller, R. (1995). From age-ing to sage-ing. New York: Warner Books.

Smith, R., & Erickson, R. (1999). Building and maintaining a strong relationship with your grandchild. [Online] Available: http://pebco.org [June 21, 1999].

Szinovacz, M. (1998). Handbook on grandparenthood. Westport, CT: Greenwood Press

University of California, Berkley, (2003). Labor projects for working families. [Online] Available: www.laborproject.berkeley.edu/familyleave/faqs.html [March 21, 2003].

U.S. Census Bureau, (2003). U.S. census 2000. [Online] Available: www.census.gov/main/www/cen2000.html [February 25, 2003].

U.S. Parks, (2003). Golden age passport. [Online] Available: www.usparks.com/misc/National_Park_fees/park_fees.shtml [February 25, 2003].

Waggoner, G (2000). Perspectives shaping and enriching the experience of aging for each member and for society. Modern Maturity, 43W(2), 85, 91.

Wassermann, S. (1996). How to stay close to distant grandchildren: The long distance grandmother. Point Roberts, WA: Hartley and Marks Publishers.

Wells, K. (1991). New god, new nation: protestants and self-reconstruction nationalism in Korea, 1896-1937. Honolulu, Hi: University of Hawaii Press.

Wendell, E. (2000). Grand-stories: 101+ bridges of love joining grandparents and grandkids. Pleasanton, TX: Friendly Oaks Publication.

Xprize.com, (2003). Lindbergh flies again.[Online] Available: www.xprize.org/education/lindbergh.html [June 10, 2003].

YMCA & Search Institute. (2002). Building strong families. [Online] Available:www.abundantassets.org [March 10, 2003].

Zullo, V. (1998). The nanas and the papas: a boomers' guide to grandparenting. Kansas City, MO: Andrews McNeel Publishing.

Soup's on . . .

Index

Yes! Send me _____ copies of
The New Face of Grandparenting . . .
Why Parents Need Their Own Parents
$14.95 each (20% discount on two or more copies)

Shipping to U.S. zip codes $4.00
Add .75 for each additional book.
Shipping to Canada or Mexico add $7.00
Overseas orders $19 U.S. funds only
Call or email for rates on multiple orders

$_____Total

Payment Method:
_____ Check/Money Order
_____ Bill my company—signed purchase order enclosed
Please charge my _____Visa _____Mastercard _____AmEx
Card # _____
Exp. Date _____

Ship to (Please Print Clearly):
Your Name _____
Address _____
City/State/Zip _____
Phone(_____) _____

Website: www.grandkidsandme.com
Email: book@grandkidsandme.com
Phone orders: 651-695-1988

Mail to:
Grandkidsandme
1764 Hampshire Ave.
St. Paul, MN 55116
USA

ISBN 0-9741710-0-X, SAN -255-3902